Sales 101: The ReadyAimSell 10-Step System for Successful Selling

By Brian Azar and Brad Fenton

ReadyAimSell

www.ReadyAimSell.com

Contents

Introduction

There is no other profession more misunderstood and likely maligned than that of smart salesmanship. With many stereotypes ablaze, can you imagine a mother saying to her child, "Bobby/Amy, you'll make Mom *so* proud one day when you become . . . a sales rep!" But, here's a little secret: nothing happens between you and your customers . . . you and your business associates . . . or with your friends and loved ones . . . *until you strike a deal— in other words, a sale is made.*

Of course, most sales trainers won't tell you anything like that. Instead, they'll try to confuse you and say that selling only happens at your job. But, in truth, that's equivalent to believing that eating only happens at a restaurant.

Stop and think about it. The world's most accomplished sales pros are selling all the time. They're selling at work . . . at home . . . while, supposedly, resting leisurely at the beach . . . and anywhere else they interact with others. But, they're not selling in the 'traditional' way; they're not using outdated, trite methods that are simply laughable by today's professional standards. In fact, after spending thousands of hours studying some of the most iconic salespeople (like the late Steve Jobs, the founder of *Apple*; Larry Ellison, the creator of *Oracle*; and Mary Kay Ash, the head of *Mary Kay Cosmetics*), we made two very alarming discoveries:

1.   The world's greatest professionals *don't appear* to be selling anything at all- In fact, you'll never catch them making any shrill pitches or initiating even a single close.

2.   Despite the fact that the world's most effective salespeople *don't appear* to be selling anything, they still manage to outsell every one of their competitors.

Now, think about it, again: Do you really believe that Steve Jobs became one of the most beloved CEOs in the world using 'old school' forms of subtle persuasion? Or what about Mary Kay Ash? Can you imagine her using 'leading questions' on national TV? Why, of course not!

The world's leading salespeople are the individuals most admired by everyone you know. They interact with thousands, even millions of people each year, and they garner the golden bucks, attract the most opportunities, and, with apparent ease, rise to the top of every profession.

And, we promise you this: You'll never catch them in the 'act' of selling! The fact is that the world's best salespeople are so caring about their product or service and clever that they don't seem to be practicing *anything* the traditional training experts teach. And, what exactly do these sales experts teach? Well, they teach *how to sell* instead of *why people buy*.

If you remember *anything* from this book, remember this: People love to buy, but they hate to be serenaded with sales or, essentially, sold to. We first learned this nugget from legendary marketing guru Freeman Gosden. He said, "If I can tell you one thing: Remember that it's not what and how you sell something that's important, it's what and how your customer wishes to buy that's important."

And that's why we teach this simple motto in all of our

seminars: *In order to sell more, you must first learn to sell less-- a whole lot less. Remember, less is more!* Sounds crazy? Well, it is crazy, *but it also works!*

A good friend of ours moved from selling custom software to marketing real estate in the most prestigious firm in all of South Florida. His shining secret? While selling software, he followed the exact opposite procedures of what everyone else in his company was doing. He focused less on selling technique and more on *why* his customers actually wanted to buy; in fact, he stopped selling altogether, and, unlike his colleagues, made it his mission to discover precisely how he could solve more problems for his customers than anyone else. He was not only a life savor, but also he reaped significantly more profits and opened up more opportunities than any other software 'salesman' in his entire firm.

Selling Less = More Sales

Honestly, we've spent years and thousands of dollars studying all of the best sales courses that we could get our hands on. We read all of the texts, listened to all of the CD programs, and attended too many seminars to count. Even more, we studied each program like a detective, methodically extracting the best techniques from each system and then applying them immediately to every situation that we could imagine.

The more we studied these programs and practiced the various techniques, however, the more frustrated we became. Why? Because nothing we found seemed to work well in the real world! In fact, most sales training programs aren't designed to work!

If you need proof, just try using an elaborate closing technique on one of your children or some 'information gathering' with your spouse. If you can't get away with those so-called skills with the people you love the most, then why on earth would you use them with your clients? Yet, that's precisely what *most* salespeople do.

They employ manipulative strategies and 'techniques' on their customers that they wouldn't dare even try with their families and friends. And, if that's not frightening enough, in a recent Gallup poll on the *honesty* and *ethical conduct* of business professionals, insurance and car salespeople were ranked at the bottom of the list!

Most people —whether we want to believe it or not— are fairly intelligent. They are not fooled by 'old school' sales techniques. It doesn't matter how clever or veiled you think that these kinds of behaviors are, since, in the mind of almost every prospect, traditional sales methods send up immediate red flags.

You probably recruit your sixth sense when you suspect you're being manipulated or lied to by a salesperson. Some professionals think that they can fool potential buyers with charm, flattery, and dramatic appeal, but these behaviors only mask their subversive motivations.

Yesterday's sales training no longer applies to modernity's fast-paced environment. What have you done to prepare yourself for today's robust competition? Have you been to any sales training seminars? Read any books on the subject?

And, if so, how current was the technology in your training, and was the material consistently tested in real-world situations?

If you are looking for techniques, suggestions, solutions, and genuine help in understanding the art of good salesmanship, then you have come to the right place. If you are searching for a quick, 'down-and-dirty' answer that tells you exactly what to say, verbatim, for practically every sales scenario that you encounter, then I suggest that you fast-forward to other sources.

Our purpose in writing this book is to help you awaken those facets of your personality that can help you to become more successful, both professionally and personally. Specifically, you will learn how to uncover areas in your patterns of thinking and behavior that prevent you from tapping into your full sales potential.

The world is full of sales resources that direct you to memorize artificial scripts, whether long and cumbersome or brief but trite. They also design scenarios that give you specific language to use in nearly every sales situation. They barrage if not inflate you with affirmation statements, and dare to teach you how to transform a prospect's 'no' into an exuberant 'yes' in minutes. If that's what you want, then you are most certainly studying the wrong book. Close this text right now, find your receipt, and return it to the bookseller immediately.

If, however, you would like to access that part of you that truly desires to master the art of effective communication and professional salesmanship, then gently put your bookmark aside, brew some coffee or tea as your sole companion and distraction, and keep on reading.

The key to benefitting from this book is understanding that you must be willing to 'tap into' your unique strengths (e.g., business, interpersonal, creative, etc.), since being a successful salesperson has much more to do with *you* than with the sales process, itself.

Chapter 1 – Saying Goodbye to the Old Game of Sales

Traditional, ego-focused selling approaches are no longer effective, because contemporary buyers are unwilling to follow you. They don't want to be 'sold to' and they want to make well-informed purchases. So, to make a sale, you must accurately identify and embrace their values.

Kevin Davis (*Getting Into Your Customer's Head)* advises us that the less you know about traditional sales tactics, then the better you'll do in the world of professional selling. You won't have abundant habits to unlearn! The worst trainees are those who think that they already know how to sell while the best students are those who are open to learning, whether neophyte or well-seasoned.

Over the years, we have observed the mistakes of many aggressive, pressure-oriented salespeople. Although their actual approaches may vary, there are many pitfalls that undermine both their business and credibility. Some of the most common include:

1. They talk instead of listening, otherwise known as 'Blabbermouth Syndrome.' Blabbermouths never sell; they merely harass others into buying an item so that they disappear from site! They erroneously assume that, if they can fill every second of silence with chatter about how marvelous their products are, then every objection in the prospect's mind will eventually disappear. But, this isn't selling at all— it's just plain irritating. Any time a salesperson is talking, a client is formulating impressions and, naturally, objections. That's just the way the human mind works. And, when

this type of salesperson takes a breath and a minute or two to listen, the customer is probably still formulating objections . . ., but, at least, he/she will have an idea about what they might be.

2. They pitch their products or services instead of asking questions. Simply said, salespeople love spouting out solutions to problems as most companies are no longer in the business of actually selling products. The greatest flaw in this approach is that too many professionals attempt to give away solutions before they even have an adequate, much less comprehensive understanding of the problem. If, instead, representatives were held accountable for their solutions, as doctors are for their prescriptions, then they would be forced to examine the problem thoroughly and ask relevant questions upfront before offering an intervention.

3. They answer *unasked* questions. When a prospect makes a statement such as, "Your price is too high," most sales professionals automatically switch into a defensive mode. Often, they begin a lengthy speech on quality or value or respond with a concession or a price reduction. But, wait. If prospects can gain a discount by merely making such a statement, then maybe they shouldn't buy yet— until they try something more powerful to get an even better price. "Your price is too high" is not a question, and it does not require an answer.

4. They fail to get the prospect to reveal a budget upfront.

How can the salesperson possibly offer a solution without knowing the prospect's priorities regarding a problem? Knowing whether there are actual funds allocated for a project will help the salesperson to distinguish between the prospect who is committed to solving a problem (action-oriented) and the one who is merely interested in 'talking about' solving the problem (contemplation-oriented). The amount of money that the prospect is willing to invest also helps to determine the most feasible and best-fit course of action.

5. They make too many follow-up calls by failing to understand that, often, the sale is already dead. Whether it is a stubborn attitude (to try and weasel every prospect into a customer) or true ignorance, too much time is spent on chasing accounts that don't qualify for a product or a service. This problem should have been detected far earlier in the sales-interview process, but we'll discuss this issue more later.

6. They fail to get a commitment to purchase *before* making a presentation. Salespeople are too willing to jump at the opportunity to showcase how clever they are by making features and benefit presentations about their products. They miss their true goal to make a sale and, unintentionally, only educate their prospects, who then have all of the information necessary to help buy from a leading competitor.

7. They small talk everything and postpone, if not skirt, the interview process. Building rapport is necessary and desirable, but, all too often, idle chat continues, and the interview process doesn't actually begin. And,

worse, the prospect usually recognizes this u-turn before the sales professional. The result is that the salesperson is back on the street wondering how he or she performed.

8. They would rather hear, "I want to think it over" than "No." Prospects are constantly ending the sales interview with the standard, "Think it over" line. The salesperson accepts this indecision and even sympathizes with the prospect as it's easier for salespeople to tell their managers that customers may buy in the future than to reveal that a prospect is just not a qualified candidate for the product. After all, wasn't it the salesperson's job to go out and find prospects to say 'yes?' Having the prospect say 'no' can also produce feelings of personal failure or rejection.

9. They see themselves as beggars instead of experts. Salespeople don't view their interviews with each customer as time spent to determine whether one qualifies to do business with their company. Instead, they usually find themselves wistfully hoping for the opportunity to 'just show my wares' and maybe, just maybe make a sale. Again, this situation is unlike the one described earlier with the physician as he or she examines the patient *thoroughly* before making a recommendation; that is, using questions as instruments to conduct a qualifying examination of the prospect.

10. They work without a systematic approach to selling.

Salespeople often find themselves improving or using a 'hit-or-miss' approach to making a sale. They allow the prospect to manage the process and often leave the scene feeling confused as they do not know where they stand. This outcome is often inevitable, because they don't know where they have been and what the next step should be. The importance of following and navigating specific steps through the process is vital to the success of a sales professional.

Do you make any of these mistakes yourself?

A Self-Evaluation Exercise: Feeling the Pressure

Here's a quick exercise. Imagine this scenario:

It's the last week of the month, and you haven't met even half of your quota. Your supervisor seems increasingly irritated by your performance, and there are three other hungry reps eager to move into your territory. Obviously, you're anxious, because your job is on-the-line, and you desperately need to make three sales before the day's end. So, here it is: It's 10:30 a.m., and you've just approached the office of your first prospect . . . . You step out of your vehicle . . . . You take your first steps toward the door . . .

Now, consider what most salespeople think about before walking through that door and approaching the prospect:

1. "Gee whiz (sigh). I hope I can make this sale . . ."

2. "I really need this sale . . ."

3. "Please! Just make 'em say, 'Yes.'"

4. "This prospect better not turn out like all the rest . . ."

5.   "All I need is the smallest hook of interest, and I know I can close this deal."

6.   "If only I had some good quality leads— prospects actually interested in what I'm offering . . ."

7.   "Where should I go eat today?"

8.   "Do I have something in my teeth?"

Or, if steeped in motivational psychology, a salesperson might be thinking:

1.   "I can do it. I can do it! Yes! By golly, I can do it!"

2.   "I like myself . . . I like myself . . . I like myself!"

3.   "I'm the 'Sales King' of the Universe!'"

So, where is the so-called sales pressure as you approach the door? On you? On your prospect? Obviously, the pressure is all on you!! And that's before you even knock on that door. Think about the implications of this approach and how it affects your prospect, and then ask yourself this question:

How would I feel about selling if there were never any pressure at all?

The New World of Pressure-Free Selling

In Aesop's fable, "The Wind and the Sun," the two characters argue over who is stronger: Seeing a traveler walking down the road, they decide to settle the issue by trying to make the visitor remove his coat. The wind takes the first turn, but, the more it blows, the more closely the traveler wraps his garments around him. Afterwards, the sun peaks and, gradually feeling its warmth, the traveler sheds his coat. The sun wins the contest.

The mindset of an 'old school' sales approach is much like the cold wind trying to force open the clenched arms of a prospect. And, despite what you may think or believe, today's consumers do have clenched arms against *whatever* tactics a salesperson says or does. But, it doesn't *have* to be this way!

The Old Game of Pressure-Selling: Another Simple Exercise

Emotions and attitudes are very powerful, and, ultimately, affect how we handle or mishandle sales situations. When you experience over-enthusiasm, pride, selfishness, anxiety, distrust, or even anger, among other feelings, you generally set yourself up for disaster operating on 'emotion-mind.'

In this exercise, look at some commonly made selling mistakes, and, more importantly, closely study the emotions surrounding them.

Part 1.

On a piece of paper folded in half, write these situations on one side of the sheet:

1.   Talking instead of listening

2.   Assuming rather than questioning

3.   Failing to fully identify the prospect's problems, needs, budget, etc.

4.   Giving up too quickly

5.   Preferring a prospect to say, "I'll think about it" rather than "No"

6.   Not answering the "What's in it for me" question from your prospect

7.   Dodging new prospects

8.   Not gaining adequate training, coaching, or support

9.   Working without a concrete plan

10.   Allowing fear to be your guide

Next, return to item # 1 and start to list the emotions and (consequent) actions that foster these types of mistakes. For example, for item # 1, you might write something like:

1. Talking instead of listening— emotions experienced:

a. Impatience

b. Frustration

c. Fear

d. Desperation

Continue down the sheet until you have followed this process for each item.

Note: When you examine all of the emotions that these pressure-oriented strategies produce, you may feel a bit overwhelmed; especially when observing how they create a vicious cycle that feeds upon itself. That's good. You *want* to associate a lot of 'pain' with these 'old school' methods of and mistakes in selling. That way, when stressful situations arise, as they always do, you won't feel so compelled to rely on familiar but wholly ineffective habits.

Part 2.

Now that you've discovered the insidious connection between these unpleasant emotions and your thoughts and behaviors, let's delve a little deeper into each of these situations. Beginning with the first situation, talking instead of listening, spend some quiet time contemplating and journaling the *negative effects* of not listening. In fact, for each of these situations, record your thoughts with devastating honesty. Here are some primers to get you started:

☆ Ask yourself a question like: *What's it like to really listen?* or *What's it like when someone's really listening to me?* For many people, the answer might start something like this: For the most part, if I'm really honest with myself, then I know that I don't really listen enough or to what's really important to the other person.

☆ You can listen for what's around you right now. Practice being mindful, and notice how many things you didn't notice until you consciously focused on listening?

☆ Or you can contemplate reality from another perspective: Have any of my friends or family members ever complained that I can be a poor listener? If so, why? If not, why? Perhaps, they're just being (too) polite.

At times, we're all closed listeners, each and everyone of us. We don't like to listen unless, of course, others are talking about us. Essentially, we love being listened to, but it can be a real challenge to authentically hear from others. It's true. Think about how many times you have ever tried to interject in a conversation or attempted to redirect someone.

Note: So now, when your colleagues, friends, or spouse ask you what you learned today, you can say: "I learned that I never really listen or listen well," and don't be too surprised if you don't get much disagreement.

Why It's Important to Associate A Lot of Pain with Old Ways of Selling

It may seem a bit somber to harp on the negative side of selling, but, over time, you'll associate more 'pain' and frustration with the 'old ways' and pleasurable, satisfying feelings with the new paradigm of pressure-free selling.

In fact, as you view your role as a traditional, 'old school' salesperson, you should consider the following:

1.   Most people you meet will not want to talk to you.

2.   Most people you meet will not like you.

3.   Most people you meet will think that you're dishonest and trying to manipulate them.

4.   Most people you meet will be agitated and, quite possibly, visibly upset.

5.   Most people you meet will then lie to you ("Oh, you've caught me at a bad time").

And, from *your* side, let's not forget:

1.   You'll get burned out in a matter of months.

2.   Your friends, loved ones, and family members will start plotting against you. After all, how can you use all of these shady tactics on your customers and not expect them or your own frustrations to affect everyone else in your life?

"But, is it really all *that* bad?" you might wonder. My answer: "Of course not." In fact, did you know that there is an upside to the 'old game' of selling? Yes, there is, and the *greatest* upside of traditional selling is that, sometimes, it actually works! Provided, of course, that your prospect is one of the following:

1.   Completely desperate

2.   Very, shall we say, uneducated

3.   Too exhausted to challenge you

I'd like you to stretch your imagination for a moment and consider a world in which selling becomes. . .

1.   fun! Yes, that's right!

2.   profitable.

3.   simple and natural; meaning, you don't have to behave one way with your clients and another way with your family and friends.

4.   something you can do without approaching burnout.

5.   and, ready for this-- immensely interesting.

Sound far-fetched? We've re-educated thousands of salespeople to see their profession in exactly this light. They not only learn to enjoy the process of selling, but also they make more revenue, create more opportunities, and find more satisfaction than they ever thought possible.

But It Does Take Some Work

Unfortunately, nothing worthwhile comes so easy. The new

methodology of pressure-free selling does require work, and lots of it, actually. Like in any profession, years and years of preparation, practice, and sacrifice are needed before really taking the stage and capturing your audience. And, as a world-class salesperson in training, you will need to devote many hours to refining your skills and unique strengths.

But (and this is a *serious* 'but'), the more diligently you work at selling *this way*, the more informed, charismatic, and magnetic you will become. Meaning, over time, most everyone you know will want to be around you more. It's like a law of attraction. What you need to ask yourself, over and over and over again, is this: *What in the world do I really want out of work and life?*

An Exercise in Self-Knowledge: Why Success?

List six or seven reasons why you want to become successful in sales.

Use the following questions to stimulate your thinking:

What's really driving you?
　　-Is it the money? (Be honest.)
　　-Do you like (or not like) working with people? (Be extremely honest.)
　　-Do you like the freedom --and responsibility-- of working for yourself?

Take a few minutes to complete this assignment now.

The 60-Second Infomercial Exercise: Who's Number 1?

This is the last but most important exercise before we move into the nuts-and-bolts tactics. It's a simple exercise but quite profound so please approach it seriously.

Scenario: Your very wealthy aunt just passed, and, instead of leaving you her fortune, she left you a 60-second commercial spot for this year's Super Bowl game. The only catch: You have to *sell yourself* in those precious seconds.

You're about to showcase yourself before close to a billion people for one full minute. This amounts to about 120 words— approximately one double-spaced page of typewritten copy. What will you say?

Remember: Honesty and sincerity are the keys to your selling success.

Remember also: Bonus points will be given for the most creative presentation.

After you've finished the assignment, move on to the next section for a three-minute evaluation of your infomercial.

Your Three-Minute Evaluation

Step 1: Take out your written infomercial and a pen.

Step 2: Read over your script, and circle the pronouns 'I,' 'me,' and 'my.'

Question 1: How many circles are on your page?

Question 2: How much relevance do you think that each of those circles has for your audience?

Tip: Hold your sheet up to the light. For every circle you see, imagine shrinking time for your pitch. . . because that's exactly what's happening as your audience is fading.

Introducing the Step-by-Step Sales Interview Approach

The old adage holds true: *The more you think about yourself, the less others think of you.* In the step-by-step sales interview that follows, you'll learn a simple but smart blueprint for pressure-free, other-oriented selling.

You'll become more like a doctor, caring for and carefully administering to your patients, rather than only caring for yourself. Following along with the strategies outlined in this book, you will not only become less stressed and infinitely more fulfilled, but also you will learn to profit from your career like never before.

In a renowned laboratory study, rats learned to run a maze differently when their prize was moved. Human beings usually have trouble 'letting go' and trying something new. But, if you keep on engaging the same way with the same results, then the time is ripe for change. Why not do something about it *now*?

Chapter 2 - Step 1: Pre-Call Planning

Standard dictionaries define the word *prospect* as a potential buyer or customer; a likely candidate. Thus, prospecting can be simply defined as the act of identifying those potential customers who are most likely to purchase your product or service. In fact, *all sales situations can be viewed as the seller looking for a buyer.*

In order to maximize their earning potential, professionals must continuously develop new customers. As seen below, the techniques of prospecting are quite diverse, but remember that, regardless of how dynamic or convincing your sales skills are, you must first find the prospect.

Being Creative

In this vein, experiment and choose those tools that work best for you. It's also important to develop techniques that apply to your specific areas. For example, when you frequently come across a particular type of stall or objection, then learn to deal with it upfront. Salespeople who have a high-priced product or service can confront objections before the client does by affirming something like, "Mr. or Ms. Prospect, I greatly appreciate your interest in my product/service, but, before we get too far, I must tell you that we are never the low bidder. Is that something we can agree on?"

Dealing with stalls and objections upfront tends to neutralize them and to alleviate pressure for both parties.

Meeting the Prospect

Before meeting your prospects, your concern should be who and where potential customers are. There are a number of sources that can aid you in discovering this critical information. Initially, you will need to research:

*Company or individual name

*Type of business/product line

*Contact information, including name, address, telephone numbers, and e-mail

*Company officers (President, CEO, etc.) and total number of employees
*Main and branch office information

This basic information assists you in understanding the prospect's business situation, and, ultimately, it can aid you in your sales interview.

For example, if you sell wireless services and are considering approaching a business that has 250 employees, then you can be certain that it has a wide variety of wireless needs. Knowing a prospect's circumstances also increases the confidence that a customer has in *you* as your careful research demonstrates concern for one's needs.

Sources for Generating Leads

Dun and Bradstreet's Million Dollar Database
www.dnbmdd.com/mddi
The resource lists approximately 39,000 U.S. companies with a net worth of $1,000,000 or more.

Standard & Poor's www.standardandpoors.com
This directory provides more than 36,000 U.S. and Canadian companies where Volume 1 supplies contact information, company officers, etc.

Chamber of Commerce Publications
Most cities have an active chamber of commerce. Contact them for lists of companies in specific industries doing business in your area.

Thomas Register of American Manufacturers
www.thomasnet.com
Furnishes a comprehensive index of American manufacturing firms; Volume 7 lists contact information, branch offices, product line history, subsidiaries, and principal officers.

State Industrial Directories
These sources provide each manufacturer by state. Data include contact information, company officers, and the number of employees.

Professional/Trade Association Directories
Physicians, attorneys, accountants, engineers, purchasing agents, and most other professionals utilize associations that list all of their members and, given annual membership, the directory is typically up-to-date.

Newspapers/Trade Periodicals
These resources are an often overlooked source of business leads—especially newspapers. In the business and public notice sections, for example, in *Crain's New York Business*, top companies and valuable 'insider information' is

published several times each year. Lists are organized into leading topics of interest such as the "500 Fastest Growing Companies in the U.S."

Internet

Virtually all of these sources and thousands more can be easily found with simple searching on the Internet. With modern techniques and a little patience, it is amazing what you can discover just by going to a company's website, especially the media and press release sections where you'll find recent activities and 'wins.'

Rules of the Road in Telephoning

If you're making your first contact by telephone, then there are a few basics that you need to keep in mind to ensure effective communication:

1.   *Attitude.* Relax, and take a few deep breaths. Establish a motivated, confident state and, as much as possible, access this mental framework each time that you pick up the phone.

2.   *Preparation.* Have your leads before you, organized in the order you plan to make your calls. Know your purpose for each call and what you will say before dialing.

3.   *Ask for Help.* Each time you make your initial contact, don't hesitate to ask for assistance. Strive for your 'Ps and Q's' by verifying important information such as spellings or pronunciations of names or gathering any other key information such as prospect's schedules and the best time to reach them.

4.   *Repeat the Prospect's First Name.* Each time you mention a contact's name, at the very least, the person will pay close attention to the next five words you say. *Listen Actively.* People who earn a living by contacting others are often the world's worst listeners. So, time to sit up and listen to those essential buying signals!

5.   *Mirror Your Prospect.* Enter your prospect's world by matching their energy level, volume, rate of speech, vocabulary, phrase construction, and mood (more about all of these factors in the later chapter on rapport). People who tend to sound like each other are more likely to appeal to each other.

6.   *Ask Qualifying Questions.* Your job is to separate prospects from suspects before making lengthy presentations. A 'qualified' prospect is one who has a need, a budget, a timeline for action, and the one who can say 'yes,' as opposed to the one who can only say 'no.'

7.   *Use Strategic Pauses.* When you ask a question or make a comment intended to elicit a response, ask and then pause for at least six seconds.

8.   *Get Specific Commitments.* Always know what is to happen next. Make sure that there is no confusion or misunderstanding by either party, including the next steps or actions to be taken.

9.   *Read Your Own Publications.* Make certain that you receive and read everything printed about your product, service, market niche, and industry.

10.   *Keep a Prospect (Contact) Database File.* For each client, keep notes on pertinent business data, follow-up, and other commentary (eg, regarding general communication style, preferred business strategies, key areas of interest, etc.) that can guide future conversations.

Setting the Mood

Look around your workspace. Is it a pleasant place to be? If not, do what you can to make it more livable. Get some plants, interesting knick-knacks, and/or pictures. Case-and-point: Make sure that there is something nearby that you enjoy looking at or using to set and encourage a positive work ethic. Get a cordless telephone; this accessibility allows you to get up, stretch, and walk around your desk uninhibited as often as needed. If possible, even get a headset. Freedom of movement allows you to feel, and, therefore, sound more relaxed and natural.

Start by memorizing the script you intend to use. Afterwards, you are free to adlib with confidence. There have been some proven rapport-building phrases and techniques incorporated into the scripts provided for you in later sections of this book. Use them, and add to them as time allows as the success of the call may depend on these first few but vital steps.

You Can't 'Sell' Anything

The key to many parts of the scripts that follow is that you are not meant to look, sound, or act like the average salesperson. Remember: The purpose of your research is *not to sell* anything. Rather, it is simply to:

1.   Gather information.

2.   'Qualify' prospects while elegantly rejecting the ones who don't.

3.   Arrange interviews with qualifying contacts.

In all cases, remember to ask for a referral! And, please, please, relax. Breathe deeply and even try to enjoy. Don't take rejection personally.

Prepare in Advance to Side-Step Put-Offs

At various stages in the direct selling process, you may have run into some common objections or stalling tactics. Here are some suggestions on how to handle them:

Prospect: Send me literature. **You:** I'd love to do that, but I wouldn't know what to send you yet. It will only take me about ten minutes to find out more specifically what information you might need, and then I should be able to provide you with everything. Do you have the time to talk now, or can you identify a time that is more convenient for me to call you? Or, **You:** Can you help me understand? What specifically are you hoping the literature will reveal to enable you to make an appointment to speak with me? (*Then deal with this issue, specifically.*)

Among other objections you might encounter:

1. Prospect: No time. We're just too busy. We won't commit [for whatever reason]. **You:** Can I ask you a personal question, off-the-record? Are the [events, machines, people, whatever your product or service] important to you?

Important enough to just invest 15 minutes of your time and my expertise? If so, great, and I'd be happy to help coordinate our calendars.

2. Prospect: We have a current supplier. **You:** I'd be concerned if you didn't have one. The reason I say that is because most of our clients currently have, or have had in the past, at least one other supplier. But, can I ask you a question? Does that mean you're closed to talking with someone who might be able to help you or your organization?

3. Prospect: We're happy with our current suppliers. **You:** Great! And does that mean that they never make a mistake, or nothing ever goes wrong? Or, **You:** Does that mean your mind is closed to talking with someone new, who may have something to help you and your organization save on costs, time, and improve [whatever area is in question]?

Sometimes, you may reach a definitive 'no.' Remember, that's not so terrible. At least, you know where you stand, and you can devote your energies to more promising prospects. You can even turn a negative into a positive. Here's how:

4. Prospect: No. Absolutely not! **You**: Gee, it doesn't look like I can help you. Maybe you can help me. Do you know anyone who might be in need of my expertise or who might need our product or service?

"Is This A Good Time To Talk?" Always remember to ask prospects if now is a good time to talk. It makes them stop what they are doing for a moment and listen to what you have to say. It shows them that you believe your call is important while demonstrating respect for their time. If a person affirms that it is not a good time, then tell the prospect that you understand and ask when would be a good time to reschedule. When you do call back, it is no longer research. You can honestly say, "Mr. Smith asked me to call at 3:00p.m." The objective is to always maintain control, and this strategy subtly helps a sales professional do just that.

Asking For Help

As noted, remember to ask for help. One of the basic premises of this selling system is that, often, people make themselves feel better by finding someone else who is not as well-off as they are. This is a sad but true finding from social comparison theory. Learning to use phrases like, "Can you help me?" and "I'm not sure" is a subtle way to hook your prospects into dropping their defenses and opening up. This approach to professional selling has been proven much more effective than the aggressive, 'know-it-all' approach. Try it out, and see how well it works for you.

When You Get To Your Prospect's Office

When you arrive at the prospect's office, don't sit in the lobby. Stand, walk around, breathe deeply, and curiously observe anything you can about the company. Pay attention to what the lobby tells you about the image that the company is trying to portray. If they spent a lot on decorating, then chances are the line, "We don't have any money" is just a stall, and, more than likely, you know that it is not really true. Take time to read the brochures that are left out for the public, and think about what they are communicating. Make sure you read any plaques or framed announcements that may be on the wall.

And, again, whatever you do, don't (passively) sit down! The physiological act puts you in a different state as your uncertainties and fears are more liable to surface when you are sunk deep into a leather sofa. Sitting can also make for an awkward first moment with your prospects as you try to get up, shake their hand, and pick up whatever you may be carrying, all at the same time. By standing, you avoid all of these irritations and put yourself on an equal level with your prospects straight from the get-go. Tell the receptionist, "No, thank you, but I've been sitting all day." Or, if it's first thing in the morning, then you might try "No, thank you, but I start early."

As you are ushered to the prospect's office or meeting place, pay careful attention to the other people you see and their surroundings. Are they pleasant or hurried, tense, withdrawn, or something else? How large is the company? Is the space clean? Do the work areas look organized? Do they have state-of-the-art equipment? This type of information can give you a great deal of insight into a company's priorities and decision-making strategies so take advantage of this 'inside look. '

Go in with nothing but yourself— no briefcase/bag, presentation materials, brochures, or anything else. Just bring your business card and a pen, and leave any other items with the safety of the front desk. By going 'naked' so-to-speak, you appear less threatening and show you are only there to talk. This stance relaxes prospects and enables them to be more open.

Remember, you are still in the information gathering stage, not the presentation stage, so you do not need to show them anything until they 'qualify.' Just assert that you customize all of your work and that, after the first interview, you will provide them with what they need. And, always, always, keep your word.

Making the First 30 Seconds Count

It is imperative to create a concise "commercial" for yourself, company, product, or service. Well-crafted, this tactic also serves to draw the prospect in by highlighting problems that you solve or major benefits that you have to offer. In essence, creating a need for your product or service-- a must before a sale can be made.

Quickly and concisely, you aim to convey the bare-bones of your offer; otherwise known as an 'elevator speech.' Start your statement with, "We are in the business of . . . ." In time, you will find that many different types of commercials are necessary, depending on the industry and audience with whom you are speaking.

Whether social, informal, or formal networking events, you can use the following ten-step procedure, which is designed to help professionals who may not be reaching the results that they want, when asked, "What do you do?"

Face-to-Face Interviews

1. Have a firm handshake.

2. Make good eye contact.

3. Smile!

4. Repeat the person's name (and remember it).

5. Ask questions to demonstrate interest and information-gather.

6. Tell them what you do (your commercial).

7. Ask more follow-up questions pertaining to how your product or service can directly benefit your prospect.

8. Exchange cards.

9. As emphasized, always, always follow up.

10. Follow Up

Using a blank sheet of paper, create a short paragraph that describes what you do via explaining the benefits of your product or service. This way, people will judge the value of your product in relationship to what they perceive it can do for them now; not what it might have done for them or others in the past. For the first draft, talk about your product or service in universal terms. This technique is especially useful when addressing groups. After you have refined it, you may wish to customize different versions to present in specific industries or markets.

Making Your Commercial

The following questions should help you to determine what benefits and solutions you want buyers to grasp when they hear about your service:

1.   What is your market?

2.   What problems are solved by utilizing your product or service?

3.   What makes you, your product, or your service unique?

Now, review questions 1–3 to notice any patterns emerging. If, over time, something keeps repeating, then it may be worth highlighting. Ask yourself what things would sound particularly powerful to a prospective customer, and write a brief paragraph that highlights why someone needs you. Start your paragraph with: "We are in the business of helping companies that may not be getting the results they want in the area of . . ."

A Few Examples

Sales Training: We are in the business of helping corporations and individuals that *may not be getting* the results they want or need in their prospecting, closing ratios, telemarketing, or revenue growth.

Life Insurance: We are in the business of helping people *who may not be getting* peace of mind, security, equity, and future financial freedom.

Commercial Real Estate: We are in the business of helping companies that *may not be getting* the benefits of current market conditions.

Residential Real Estate: We are in the business of helping individuals *who may not be getting* the results they want from the marketing, advertising, and servicing their current agents are providing.

Caterer: We are in the business of helping organizations *that may not be getting* that personal touch that they want and need in the catering of their private parties or corporate affairs.

Freelance Illustrator: We're in the business of helping individuals *who may not be getting* the image they want in their brochures, on their letterheads and business cards, and in their advertising, to assist them in more clearly projecting their mission and values.

Computer Consultant: We are in the business of helping companies *that might not be getting* the results they want in terms of employee productivity, information monitoring, and communication between departments.

Telecommunications/Data Transmission: We are in the business of helping individuals *who may not be getting* the rates, services, or reliability they need from their current vendors

Questions Are The Answer

By far, questioning is the most important skill to develop as a master sales professional. The processes of elegant questioning and information gathering are paramount to a 'Ready-Aim-Sell philosophy.' It is what sets you apart from the dreaded used car dealer stereotype. Pay particular attention to this section, and practice the techniques outlined within. They will become an integral part of your selling script as, indubitably, the success of your entire sales track depends on effective questioning skills.

We have often maintained that your success in selling is directly proportional to the amount of information that you *don't* give away for free. In other words, *telling* isn't *selling*. For you to stop selling and simply allow people to buy, you must learn how they want to be sold to. They will tell you, but you need to know how to listen, and how to ask germane questions. Remember, you have two ears and one mouth for a reason. On a sales call, you should be listening twice as much as you speak, and, when speaking, you should be asking questions.

The Ten Rules of Questioning

1. Most prospects lie. If you ask the average person to describe salespeople, they will most likely utilize words like *loud, pushy, obnoxious, insensitive, even liars,* and the like. It's no wonder a salesperson is most often perceived as impolite and either impersonal or inappropriately friendly. So, as described, it's easy for prospects to lie, because, in many cases, professionals have legitimized these practices: "He's in a meeting," "I'm too busy," "Send me the literature," "I'll think about it." These lines are all defense mechanisms that customers have developed against the stereotype of a salesperson. But, don't hold it against them, just understand it, and deal with it.

2. During a call, forget most of the advice that your mother taught you; rules like, "Don't talk to strangers" and "When I ask you a question, answer me!" are just some examples to go by the wayside.

3. Put your ego aside. In order to be successful, we all need to be confident and prepared. Your prospects will sense if you are not, and, worse, they will question your credibility. As noted, it is important to ask for help so don't be afraid to say "I'm not sure" and "Can you help me?" These two questions can be used to gather information, diffuse resistance, and, ultimately, to build rapport.

4. Stop talking your way out of sales and start questioning your way in. As an educated professional, it's natural to want to demonstrate your knowledge as much as possible. But, wait! Stop giving it away! Stop talking, and start asking. Get consumers to clarify exactly what they want to know. It's your job to ask pointed questions that zero-in on their concerns, needs, budget, and decision-making policies— before you start your presentation. That means, on the first call! Be prepared to say statements like, "Gee, you're on page 12, and I'm still on page 1," or, "Can you help me? I need to get some more information before I can properly answer that."

5. When you're talking, you're not selling. Listen. Listen. Listen! This is the most vital part of questioning. Remember what you are trying to achieve. The whole purpose of questioning is to encourage your prospect to open up and to talk so breathe deeply or bite your tongue if you have to, but *keep your prospect talking.* An open-ended but affirming comment like, "Oh?" gives them no choice but to expound on what they have said.

6. To put the shoe on the other foot, remember the 'rule of three questions.' Don't assume that you know why your customer is asking a question. Even a simple question can have hidden significance. For example: "Do you sell a lot of these?" could get you into trouble if handled incorrectly. If you just say, "Yes," you might be surprised to hear, "I'm sorry to hear that. I was looking for something unique."

However, if you say, "Gee, that's an interesting question; why do you ask?" the dialogue might continue. The prospect might answer, "Well, because I want to know how many you sell." Then you could say, "That makes sense, but tell me why that's important to you."

When the prospect replies, "Because I'm looking for something unique," you can manage the issue or suggest an alternative without getting backed into a corner. Remember to use softening statements like, "That makes sense," or "That's an interesting question," before your real question so that prospects don't feel that they're being drilled.

7. Turn the tables. In order to maintain control of the interview, you still have to be the one asking the questions. So remember to end every answer with another question. Something like, "Does that sound like something you'd be interested in?" or, "Is that a fair statement?" can help you finish qualifying or, if needed, to gather more information. Keep the ball rolling at all times, but be natural or, to put it plainly, you'll just sound pushy.

8. Keep in mind that statements aren't questions. If you answer a question that hasn't been asked, you could cause antagonism by sounding like you're defending yourself. This means that you have to put your ego aside, again, because you won't always agree with your prospect. But, it's all part of being a professional.

Specifically, "It's too expensive!" does not require an answer, but acknowledge it is a sign of resistance. When confronted, always follow the three *flo-with steps* or, in another words, *roll-with,* steps: (1) Agree (2) Insert the word *and* (3) Ask another question to maintain the communication.

9. If they ask the same question twice, then be sure to answer it. However, you don't want to offend anyone with too many questions. So be sensitive to your prospect's attitudes and non-verbal emotions. A good rule is that, if they repeat the same question twice, then answer it, or it will appear as if you're ignoring them. But, don't be afraid to reject a prospect who refuses to answer any questions or who takes too much of your time to qualify successfully. Part of being a master sales professional is knowing that you won't qualify or close every prospect. In fact, rejecting them is sometimes part of maintaining your control.

10. Be natural. It's a good idea to hesitate before you answer a question. This shows that you consider the question worthy of thought, and it helps you to avoid sounding like you are working directly from a script. With regards to all of the questioning that we suggest in this book, tone and tempo are very important. Practice making them sound natural. Use a mirror, or do some role-playing with a colleague.

Your job is to qualify leads as quickly as possible in order to make an appointment or to remove the person or company from your system. Remember, an unqualified file is an unknown. Develop the attitude that the lead needs to prove its value in order to warrant space in your box or computer. Your success will be determined as much by the number of files you tear up or delete as by the number of *hot* prospects that you secure.

Chapter 2/ Step 1 Summary

1. Memorize the "Telephone Rules of the Road." They are designed to slide you into a comfortable, productive relationship with your prospects:

☆ Be Prepared

☆ Convey a confident and motivated attitude

☆ Listen actively

☆ Repeat the prospect's first name

☆ Ask qualifying questions

☆ Mirror your customer

☆ Use the 'strategic pause'

☆ Ask for help

☆ Get specific commitments

2. Pay attention to your prospect to really focus your listening and to carefully monitor your own reactions and behavior.

3. Remember the 'Ten Rules of Questioning':

(1) Forget your mother's advice.

(2) Most prospects lie.

(3) Put your ego aside.

(4) Stop talking your way out of sales, and start questioning your way in.

(5) Realize that, when you're talking, you're not selling.

(6) Remember the 'Rule of Three.'

(7) Turn the tables.

(8) Keep in mind that statements aren't questions.

(9) If they ask the same question twice, then answer it.

(10) Finally, always be natural- be yourself as much as possible

Chapter 3 – Step 2: Establishing Rapport

Establishing rapport is indisputably one of the most important —and intricate— aspects of the sales interview process. Executed with care and precision, relationship building makes each subsequent step easier and more likely to yield successful results. If undervalued, however, the outcomes can be disappointing; at worst, contaminating the possibility of a relationship by ushering feelings of disdain, mistrust, or other conflict. It's not necessarily a difficult skill set to attain, but, among other factors, its art requires open-mindedness, patience, focused concentration, and timing.

This chapter intends to provide a treasure chest of information that will give you perspective on the rapport-building process, along with tools, techniques, and some self-administered exercises to help you understand yourself and the consumers to whom you are selling.

Getting Over to Your Customer's Side of the World: An Introduction to Rapport

Most salespeople believe that bonding is rapport and that you must connect with your customers before you can move forward. There is a difference, however:

Bonding: Where you, the professional salesperson, initially lead the talking to find a common thread with your prospects; making them feel comfortable while you talk and they listen.

Rapport: Where you ask the prospects a question about something positive related to their company, ideology, or service, and they do the talking while you listen. This way, you can mirror and pace them by entering into their unique phenomenological space.

The early steps of rapport building with your clients could be the most important and, perhaps, the most challenging aspects of the sales process.

At this stage, your goal is to create a feeling of similarity between you and your prospect. We are all drawn to those whom we perceive to be like ourselves, but, to establish rapport as well as credibility and trust, you must take the time to set the tone of the call by tapping your finest mirroring skills.

You might start your communication by asking your prospects to share some information about themselves and how they arrived at where they are today. Remember, people enjoy talking about themselves so fancy them and listen. If you are genuine in your interest and enthusiasm, this technique can be a solid rapport builder. And, in the course of listening, if you find that you have something in common (e.g., like living in the same town or having gone to the same school), that thread can also assist you.

The following are some ice-breaking suggestions that you may want to use.

Scenario One

You: I'm so glad we were able to talk today. Before we get started, I was wondering if you could just share some general information about [ABC Company], such as how long you've been in business, the kind of growth you've been experiencing and expecting, and so forth.

Of course, you should already know this information from your pre-call information gathering (as discussed in the previous chapter), but this introduction gives customers the opportunity to discuss a familiar subject and creates a point of connection.

Prospect: (Responds) **You:** That's very interesting. I wasn't aware that such a large market existed for timesharing. If you don't mind me asking, I'm curious about how you arrived at your current position as . . .

OR

You: That's very interesting. I wasn't aware that such a large market existed for timesharing. If you don't mind me asking, I'm always curious about how successful people like yourself actually arrive at their current positions. Would you be willing to share that with me?

Prospect: (Responds)

You: On that note, just one last question before we get down to business: If you could pinpoint one quality that has made you unique in your approach, what would it be?

Scenario Two

You: Thanks for talking with me today. During this time, I'll be asking you some questions. After, you'll have time to ask me whatever follow-up questions you'd like, and then we can decide if we have the basis for a beneficial relationship. Are you okay with that?

Prospect: Sure.

You: Before we begin the conversation, (of course, the 'real conversation' has already begun), I wonder if you would share some information about ABC Company, including your influential role at ABC. How did ABC start? What has your role been in its growth? And what is your vision for ABC's future?

Neuro-Linguistic Selling Skills (NLSS)

The use of neuro-linguistics, the study of how people communicate, is an extremely powerful way to subtly create a feeling of similarity between you and your prospect. Everyone has different communication channels, and, if you can identify and tune into these primary modes, then you can obtain much better results and shorten the entire sales cycle.

To truly understand the field and benefits of neuro-linguistics, it is important to first grasp the basic elements of communication or, subconsciously, what exactly it is that makes a person feel comfortable with another. These steps can be broken down in the following fashion:

55 % Physiology
Breathing patterns, Gestures, Facial expressions, Mirroring

38 % Tone
Speech tempo, Volume, Voice quality, Timbre

7 % Words
Content: Common experience, Key words and phrases

To give you an illustration of how this phenomenon occurs in your everyday communication, try this exercise: Remember a time when you were a young child and were reprimanded for something. The parent or adult who confronted you began by saying your name. Then, as you mustered the courage to look up and heard the person's voice, you instinctively knew that you were 'in trouble' and understood why. But, how come? All he/she did was call your name.

Well, your name, of course, accounted for 7 %. But, the way your name was pronounced and the posture and expression of the caregiver revealed far more than the words ever could. As a matter of fact, we would like to suggest that, even as a small child, you clearly understood what was happening, maybe not through words, but by using all of your senses. Children are remarkably clever and can detect and interpret basic emotions (eg, fear, anger, sadness, joy) long before speaking.

The same is true for adults. You don't just hear the words your prospect uses to determine your performance on a sales interview. How many times have prospects told you that they were really interested, but they just had to think it over... for a little while longer? You heard their verbal response, but, at the same time, you knew it was over and that they had already decided against it.

When we listen mindfully, we are unconsciously absorbing information with all of our senses. Similarly, when we express ourselves, we not only employ words but also kinesics and all forms of non-verbal behavior.

Good communication can be defined as instrumental; meaning, obtaining the results you desire in order to achieve your goals. Neuro-linguistics, while seemingly complex, displays its brilliance best in the way that it analyzes and applies to functional communication. With this critical understanding of a new science, you can start creating the subtle changes that will make a significant difference in your ultimate results.

The following are the three main sensory channels that we rely on when communicating and the approximate percentage of the population that depends most on each sense.

Video (seeing): 60 %

Audio (hearing): 25 %

Kino (feeling): 15 %

In addition, there are also the olfactory (smelling) sense, the gustatory (tasting) sense, and intuition (our sixth) sense. At any given moment, one of these channels is likely to have a greater 'signal strength' than the others. We all, however, tend to rely on one sense more than the others given personal preference and learning style.

We believe that intuition is the most powerful sense modality. Because many people don't understand its importance, it is largely ignored. However, it is becoming much more recognized in some circles, notably in the corporate sector. This realization will create many changes for 'big business' in the decades to come.

The olfactory sense is extremely powerful in its ability to transport you to another place or time. No sense can recreate a poignant feeling or memory faster than that of smell. For example, have you ever smelled a particular food that your mother used to make? Immediately, childhood images can come to life. In fact, you cannot only smell it, but also you can see, hear, feel, and taste it. It's like you are literally there! This is a fine example of anchoring in a neuro-linguistic-induced state. The increased use of aromatherapy is testimony to how much we've learned about the power of this sense and the effectiveness of applying that knowledge.

For the purpose of selling, let's focus on the most recognized and principal senses: *video, audio,* and *kino.* These are the senses most often used, and people naturally rely on one more than the others. As seen above, most people rely on video input, or what we call *primary videos,* and, in sales interviews, it is important to try to determine the best match for your prospect. This way, you can communicate more effectively using the cues to which they are most responsive.

For example, for individuals who are oriented towards primary videos, they want to *see* your product and *read* your brochures, literature, and testimonials. Customers who are oriented towards primary audios, by contrast, prefer to *hear* you advertise the product details, benefits, and others' reviews. Finally, people who are oriented towards the kino method prefer to sample your product to 'get the feel of it' while evaluating its utility.

Most people have more than one strategy, but, as

emphasized, it is important to recognize their primary one. For example, if you are a fast-talking, visual person and you are trying to communicate with someone who relies on an auditory strategy, then you probably won't get through. Remember the teachers you had in school who made you consistently drift into a soft slumber? In reality, they probably were not so much 'boring' as too little oriented towards your keen kinesthetic sense.

You can begin to read your prospects by listening to the language they use. Below are some commonly used words or phrases that others employ to relate their experiences through video, audio, or kino processes:

Video –see, look, appear, an eyeful, bird's eye view, in view of, eye-to-eye, make a scene, clear-cut
Audio – hear, listen, sounds like, express yourself, idle talk, inquire into, loud and clear, tuned in, word-for -word, unheard of
Kino – sense, feel, contact, grasp, cool and calm, boils down to, hold it, hang in there, get the drift, get in touch

The use of any of these words or phrases does not necessarily indicate a person's sensory channel preference. However, it is important to pay close attention to all of the words that people use in order to deduce their general processing style.

Along with what is said (7 %), you must attend to delivery and to key physiological indicators. Here are some guidelines that you can follow to identify the three chief sensory channels typically utilized by right-hand dominant individuals.

Primary Video (60 %)

Primary video-oriented people tend to speak very rapidly. They also gesticulate a lot as they speak while peering at the field of view directly ahead of them. They think in pictures and actually visualize these images in front of them.

Remember when you were in school and a teacher exclaimed to you or a peer, "The answer is not on the ceiling!" Well, for primary-oriented video students, the answer actually was on the ceiling! In general, video types look up and to their right when creating and up and to their left when they remember.

Their breathing is shallow (often very high in their chest), and, when they get excited, they may almost hyperventilate. They say things like, "I see," "I get the picture," "It looks good," and "That's not what I envision." They usually make quick decisions, tend to be very manicured dressers, and are concerned about the appearance of almost everything. Their desks and living areas also tend to be neat and orderly, and they often believe what they read or observe.

Primary Audio (24 %)

Primary audio-oriented people tend to talk at a moderate rate, although, strangely, their voices are usually more monotonous than primary video-oriented individuals. In general, they are very even-tempered with relaxed breathing patterns and posture to match.

Primary audio-oriented sensors would likely read information aloud and repeat it continuously when studying for an exam. They talk to themselves to mediate ideas or, especially problems, and hear thoughts running like a daily chronicle in their mind. They tend to look from side-to-side a lot as they think and speak, and, in general, they look to their right when producing and to their left when recalling. They also think horizontally, as if reading words from a page.

They commonly say phrases like, "That rings a bell," "I like the sound of that," "Tell me more," and "I don't think I'm hearing you correctly." They have a tendency to believe what you say and what they hear (whether or not it matches).

Primary Kino (15 %)

Primary kino-oriented learners are probably the most misunderstood of the three types. They tend to talk rather slowly, and their tone and volume are usually more deliberate and quiet. They are used to getting cutoff when speaking, because others don't want to wait for them to finish. Generally, they are also very mellow and prefer to get a 'feel for things' before acting, so they may take more time to make decisions.

Kino-oriented individual are more in touch with their intuition than any other group. They, therefore, tend to interpret situations more personally and are vulnerable to rejection. They feel the weight of the world on their shoulders and may be more sensitive to stress, saying say things like, "I have to get a handle on the situation," "My feeling is this," and "I'm beginning to grasp the idea" when confronting too many or, possibly, complex demands.

They look down and to the right a lot, breathing from deep in their diaphragm, and they tend to not only wear but also to surround themselves with comfortable belongings. They like to touch and be touched, and, in general, they are very warm, gentle, and caring.

Now that you have a basic understanding of the range of behavior that you can encounter, think about how your communication with different types of people can be affected and enriched. A video- or audio-oriented person, who is not responsive to the methods of a fellow kino, undoubtedly finds it challenging and, perhaps, even unpleasant to communicate with one; where the reverse is also true.

In sales, our job is to communicate freely and effectively with all types of prospects. When you are able to determine your prospects' primary sensory channel, you will be able to adapt your communication to *their* personal style. Give them what they respond to best by showing, telling, or helping them to 'get a feeling' for your subject matter; in this case, your product or service. Ask them relevant questions that demonstrate you understand how they think as well as their unique processes of evaluation and decision-making. "What would you have to [see, hear, or experience] today or in the near future to make a good decision?" Talk to them on *their* level, and they'll not only want to work with you but also to refer you.

Now that you have a basic understanding of the range of behavior that you can encounter, think about how communication with different types of people can be affected. You can do this by *mirroring* and *matching*.

Mirroring and Matching

Remember, if we try to create rapport with only the content of our conversation, then we are missing out on one of the most important ways that we can communicate similarly to another person. Mirroring, which is the act of adopting another's behavior as if you were that person's mirror image, is the key.

Mirroring requires two tools: keen attention and personal flexibility. On the telephone, it means that you must also be able to identify and match others' (verbal) attitudes, expressions, tone, and, in general, pace their speech. If performed subtly, you will increase your ability to foster strong rapport.

These dual strategies, working hand-in-hand, have two payoffs. As you mirror, the person is likely to think, "Hey, this guy/gal is like me! He/she must be okay!"

Second, mirroring literally gives you the opportunity to briefly place yourself into someone else's shoes and allows you to communicate from *another side of the world*.

Sales Tip!

When you first introduce yourself and ask a question, just start by mirroring. Once forming this critical connection, move subtly to understanding their entire process utilizing neuro-linguistic cues. If a prospect talks slowly, then definitely pace yourself, or, if speaking softly, do the same. If you find that you are losing a customer's attention, then just repeat the mirroring process until a connection is formed. Once you solidify it, remember that it's helpful to breathe and just be yourself as we all prefer to do business with people who understand our needs and share our worldview.

Phrase Construction

Listen carefully to the pattern of the prospects' speech and respond in kind. Some people speak in short, choppy sentences while others communicate in long, drawn-out phrases. If prospects interrupt you frequently, then they may think in short phrases and/or even be impatient with your detail-focus. Try shortening your form. By contrast, if prospects repeatedly ask you for more explanations, then they may be curious, skeptical, or simply more comfortable with longer accounts.

Volume

Match your volume with the person as many representatives make the common mistake of nearly shouting when trying to urge consumers to speak louder. What usually happens is that prospects respond by lowering their voices to get the salesperson to listen! The result is frustration on both ends of the line.

However, if you lower your volume to match that of someone who is soft-spoken, then that person will feel more comfortable conversing with you. And, never, never automatically assume that older prospects have hearing difficulties as raising your voice may only offend them.

Vocabulary

Listen to and repeat the words your prospect uses, whether or not their language is entirely appropriate. In selling a service or a product to a computer enthusiast, for example, you will access a completely different vocabulary from what you would use when selling the same item to an avid sports fan.

The best way to navigate your prospects' working vocabulary is through active listening skills and the creative use of open-ended questions. Mark down key words and phrases as they speak, and use them appropriately throughout the conversation and for future callbacks.

Rhythm and Rate of Speech

Adjusting your rhythm and rate of speech also helps you to avoid preconceived judgments that can interfere with rapport building.

Moods

Without actually adopting the mood of your prospects, match the pace of your energy to theirs. If you are very effervescent when you place a call to those who are serious and somber, then establishing rapport will be quite unlikely. In this example, by briefly pacing and matching their low energy level, you can be more flexible in offering perspective and, through gradual reinforcement, subtly shift their mood.

When you are able to determine your prospects' primary sensory channel, give them what they will respond to best. Create mental pictures, explain and define ideas, or help them 'get a feeling' for your product or service.

Sales Tip!

Although this section provides a good overview of neuro-linguistics, we highly recommend that you study this science further in order to make the best use of it. Neuro-linguistics can be both fascinating and very productive in your personal and professional life.

Have fun with this valuable new tool!

What is Your Own Personal Style?

Once you identify your processing style, it will help you to better understand how you sense, interpret, and convey information in business and communicative interactions, in general. You will also feel less overwhelmed and more confident.

By discovering all of the factors that make *you the way that you are*, you will have more energy to invest in observing and understanding prospective clients' modes. You will learn how to maneuver these elaborate systems to benefit both your client and, ultimately, you as a salesperson.

For example, the next time that you have a meeting, take an inventory of what people around the room are actually doing:

☆ Do you see them wandering around the room with their eyes?

☆Are people expressionless and listless?

☆Perhaps, while you were giving your presentation, the man in the far corner was doodling for 15 minutes.

When people are not stimulated by your primary style, they become antsy and apathetic. If you are speaking with visual people, then don't bore them with stacks of statistical data. They need to connect with pictures so give them a chart with bright colors and graphics.

Likewise, if you plan to meet with so-called 'warm and fuzzy' types, then they will need to feel like you are connecting before they can even begin 'talking business.' Rushing into your presentation will turn them off quickly so, instead, ask them a lot of questions. Find out what they are thinking, and gradually show them your information to help them 'connect' with you during the presentation. Their eye contact, facial expressions, and gestures will help you to accurately assess your performance.

And, again, remember that, just because you have a primary communicative mode doesn't mean that, depending on the circumstances and issues you encounter, you won't be able to adjust your style by relying more on one than another. Just practice, practice, practice to be able to adapt 'on-your-feet.'

Neuro-Linguistic Review

Selling to a Visual Prospect

With these customers, even mental pictures are truly worth

a thousand words! Of course, visual materials, whether samples, photos, videotaped materials, slides, relevant charts, or the like, are all instrumental.

Also, rely on visual expressions: "Does this *look good* to you?" "Have I made that *clear?*" "*Imagine* what that could mean to your company."

In your close, lead your prospect through a review of benefits as though broadcasting a television drama. Use their imagination to picture the agreement that you've reached, and make sure the prospects "see" the contract in their mind's eye.

Speaking artfully, carefully, and crafting mental images is crucial to succeeding with highly visually-oriented consumers.

Selling to an Auditory Prospect

Use testimonials and endorsements. Since they think with words rather than pictures or feelings, they are likely to be attracted to quotations and other parenthetical support.

Mirror their way of speaking. Use similar vocabulary, cadence, pacing, and volume, but with subtle finesse so that they don't know they're being imitated. At the same time, vary aspects of your communication style reflected in your tone, volume, and speech rate to emphasize and verbally punctuate your most important points. Auditory people pay as much attention to your delivery as to the content of what you say.

Sprinkle in audio-oriented words: "Does that *sound good* to you?" "Are we in *harmony* on that point?" "Do I need to *amplify* anything we've covered?" In addition to visual or print brochures, which often end up unread or thrown away, definitely call them on the phone frequently. Even a brief conversation can revive interest or serve as a clincher to make that sale.

Selling to a Kinesthetic Prospect

Use words that suggest physical action and harbor emotional appeal: "How do you *feel* about the proposal?," "Are you *comfortable* with these options?," and "I want to get a *handle* on your exact requirements." Since you can't actually establish physical contact, use words that evoke emotional attachment and that create positive feelings about your product or service.

Customers will be more likely to perceive you as enthusiastic and genuine. If you choose your words carefully, kinesthetic prospects will intuitively know that you care very much about what you actually say.

Sales Tip!

1.   Step back and notice those people, in both personal and professional settings, with whom you have solid rapport and those with whom you lack strong connection. What is the difference between these two groups?

2.   What do you need to know about an individual in order to establish greater rapport— or, perhaps, rapport at all? What specifically makes it difficult for you to be with

these types? What would *they* have to do or how would they need to think differently *for you* to approach, if not accept them? Stretch yourself further and consider some behaviors that you would have to adopt in order to try and accept them.

3.   Now, examine your client base. Are these some of the same people with whom you have a difficult time? Consider any non-verbal similarities that you could gravitate towards to help you create rapport with them.

4.   During your calls, attempt to 'voice match' immediately through factors such as your volume, tone, tempo, and pitch. Although this is a conscious process for you, realize that the person on the other end won't notice anything other than a feeling of sameness. Continue only until necessary or when critical rapport is reached:

A. It may take a while, but you will recognize this point of connection when the conversation becomes more fluid. You will be less aware of 'trying to do anything different' from whom you are naturally.

B. Maintain a 'we space' by working from a point of agreement and continually summarizing the information that you've gathered.

C. Internally, always monitor your client's comfort level. Has his/her tempo or volume changed? Are the two of you regularly turn-taking?

Chapter 3/ Step 2 Summary

Create rapport at the earliest but most natural moments during a call. But remember, words only comprise 7% while supra-segmental features of the voice constitute 38% and physiology affects 55% of communication.

Through *mirroring* and detecting language clues, determine whether your prospect is a *primary video-, audio-, or kino-oriented person* and learn to adapt your communication style accordingly. Continue using mirroring and matching strategies to create and, once established, to reinforce rapport.

The *old* game of sales —involving persuasion, manipulation, frustration, and control- takes a lot of work for both you *and* your customers. The new game of pressure-free selling —incorporating inquiry, connection, and commitment— may also be labor-intensive, but, at least, it's relatively burden-free by entering your consumer's world rather than forcing them into yours.

Chapter 4 – Step 3: Finding the Pain

Let's imagine that you go for your annual checkup, and, at your appointment, your doctor says, "Boy, am I glad you're here today— we've got a special on kidney stone removal— whaddya say?" Aghast, you answer, "But, Doc, my kidneys are just fine. No problems there."

And the doctor replies, "Oh, really? Well, then, how about a tonsillectomy— we're running a discount on that, too, and, you know us, we do excellent work. I mean, just ask anyone! How about it?" By now, you'd probably be careening out of the door and headed to filing a malpractice (or crazy) claim!

Clearly, the doctor didn't bother to ask what *you needed* before trying to sell services that had no relevance to you. Sound completely absurd? Exaggerated to make a point— absolutely. But, as sales professionals, what do we do often do?

Yes! So, forget what other people have told you, and don't begin a sales interview with your presentation. Why? Because it's the same as a doctor recommending an intervention before diagnosing the ailment. It just makes zero sense!

Additionally, when calling a prospect, think of yourself as a *sales doctor*. Remember that people don't usually purchase to gain features or benefits. The real reason that they buy is to alleviate or to avoid challenges; in other words, to reduce problems that create 'pain' and conflict in their lives. As soon as prospects realize that you have the cure for the 'pain' (specifically, their 'pain'), they'll close the sale themselves.

Instead of making a presentation, ask open-ended questions following a very specific sequence:

1. First, you want to *find* the 'pain'— the prospect's problem/s.

2. Then, you want to *qualify* the patient or prospect.

3. Finally, you want to *propose* the cure (making your presentation).

And, remember, never make the presentation until you've gone through the first two steps. Because, do it too soon, and, although the patient may not die, the sale will!

This approach is the most powerful and effective method of selling in the contemporary marketplace. All it requires is sharp interviewing skills (eg, rapport building, questioning) and an understanding of a very basic concept.

Highly effective representatives know how to examine their prospects in a similar way that a doctor would. A practitioner assesses the source of the 'pain', formulates and communicates the diagnosis, recommends an intervention, and initiates a treatment plan. You'd be amazed at how little time most sales professionals and other entrepreneurs really spend on asking prospects about their concerns and needs. So, play the doctor role with your prospects and just see how differently they respond. And, just in case, bring some smelling salts when you find yourself astonished!

Finding the Pain

Think of yourself as a sales doctor from the very beginning

of the call. Start with the kind of conversation that puts the customer at ease and establishes rapport. Then, question the prospect just as a physician would interview a patient to uncover and diagnose the symptoms.

Ask open-ended inquiries such as, "How is your present system (or service)?" Depending on the answers you obtain, move from there to specifics— perhaps, "What don't you like about it?," "What problems have you had?," or "If you could change one thing, what would it be?" As the prospect responds in kind, listen carefully. One of the worst mistakes that most sales professionals make is talking *too* much. If you're over-talking, you're out of control and, even worse, you're definitely not selling.

With active listening, they become your captured audience and begin revealing their 'pain'. But remain patient and wait on the prescription. You still don't have enough information to work with, and you need to dig and probe with more detailed questions. The surgeon's tool is the scalpel, and the sales professional's tools are various questions that are designed to facilitate disclosure.

Elaborate with, "Is there anything else you need to tell me?" or "You mentioned your concern about (whatever). Can you tell me a little more about that?" Keep digging. Keep probing. Here are some other questions that may be useful:

☆"How long have you been looking for . . .?"

☆"Is size important?"

☆"Do you have any particular concerns relating to . . .?"

☆"Is there anything about your present system that you particularly like?"

☆"Is there anything that you particularly dislike?"

Sometimes your prospects (patients) may not fully realize that they have a problem to solve; especially without obvious symptoms to report. In these more difficult cases, it is necessary to probe for the 'pain'. If you were selling testing kits, for example, it might sound something like this:

Scenario One

You: How is your present testing system working for you? **Prospect:** Fine. **You:** When you say "fine," what, specifically, do you mean? **Prospect:** Well, the tests are inaccurate sometimes, but, overall, they're okay.

You: So, if they were more precise, you'd be completely happy with it? Is that a fair statement? **Prospect:** Well, no, not exactly. **You:** Why not? **Prospect:** Well, after we catch an error, the next twenty or so tests require extra checking, which means repeating them. **You:** Oh, I see. And, what happens when you re-do the tests? **Prospect:** Well, it takes time. Sometimes it's messy, and it takes longer to get the job done. **You:** Gee, how do you feel when that happens? **Prospect:** Terrible! The real work isn't getting done, because they're playing with the equipment! And, the boss thinks they're poorly managed and goofing off.

Now that you finally know the origin of the real 'pain', prepare yourself and the prospect for the presentation (operation) by asking: **You:** If you could create the quintessential test, what would you hope to gain? What would it do for you personally to help you perform on the job?

Scenario Two

You: How is your present testing system working for you?
Prospect: Fine. **You:** When you say "fine," what specifically, do you mean?

Prospect: It works fine. I'm happy with it.

You: Let me ask you this. On a scale from '0 to 10,' 10 being the best, how productive would you say your testing system is? **Prospect:** Oh, I'd give it a solid 8. **You:** OK, and what would it take for the system to be a perfect 10?" **Prospect:** Well, it would have to be a system that didn't fail so often and wouldn't require so much checking and calibration.

You: Oh, I see. It sounds like you don't have that kind of system now. Is that a fair statement? **Prospect:** Yes, that's fair to say. **You:** How do you feel about losing 20 % in productivity? **Prospect:** Honestly, not too good. It's probably costing me money in the long-run. **You**: So, if there were a cost-effective way to bring your testing and productivity up to 10, would that interest you? **Prospect**: Why, sure. Anybody would be interested in that.

After cleverly uncovering three or more challenges ('pains') that your prospect is coping with, it is important to determine the intensity of each 'pain.' In other words-- what hurts most, least, and in-between. It might sound something like this:

You: In order to be sure that I heard you, correctly, I'd like to review your list of concerns with you. You seem upset about the frequent failure rate. The service tech usually doesn't get there until the next day to check the equipment so, unfortunately, the system isn't really designed to handle emergency requirements. So, in these situations, you end up sending material out for testing. And, except for one person, no one can really figure out how to operate the calibrator. Did I address all of your concerns— does that sound right?

Prospect: Yes. I'd say you got it.

You: Okay. And which of those issues is most pressing?

Continue in this manner until you have the prospect's concerns in order of importance and can actually construct a list of priorities.

A Quick Example

Steve Henderson landed an impressive sales job working for a leader in the packaged goods food industry. One of his first sales calls was with a buyer from a major supermarket chain. Steve wanted to convince the buyer to take on a line extension that the food company was introducing. Steve had enjoyed many years as a successful salesperson and used a 'tried and true' presentation with lots of bells and whistles, plenty of audiovisual props, and a stack of statistics.

This sales strategy had helped Steve to rack in tons of new clients for previous employers. He even earned salesman of the year for three years in a row. When Steve delivered his presentation to the prospect, the buyer appeared a little uncomfortable with the pitch. Steve assumed that the client's attitude was attributable to the fact that he was new on the job and since they had no prior relationship.

At the end of his presentation, the buyer asked Steve a few questions, and, when he jumped for the sale, the buyer said he'd get back to him. Guess what? The buyer never did, and Steve's attempts to 'touch base' were hindered by reception or running voicemails. He tried reaching the buyer at an off time to see if he could catch him before the start of the workday, and he did. The buyer politely noted that he really didn't have the shelf space for the new line so the decision would be postponed for some time.

After some reflection, Steve discovered that he might have overwhelmed the buyer. In fact, he admitted that his anxiety prevented him from focusing on the buyer's non-verbal messages and listening much more attentively to his individual needs.

Specifically, Steve remembered that the sales manager had mentioned that shelf space was tight prior to his presentation, yet he neglected to address this critical problem (symptom cluster) and, instead, 'went in for the kill.' He was more concerned with closing the deal than he was with understanding the buyer's unique needs and providing a solution for his customer's 'pain' point.

Steve realized that he should have prepared a presentation around the *'pain' point* and then gradually, strategically negotiated for the space. Once formally preparing his thoughts, he wrote the prospect a letter that focused on solving his customer's major 'pain' point— limited shelf space. Steve also referenced several trade deals that his company had previously used for line extensions and which proved to supply valuable benefits for retailers. With greater confidence, the buyer called a few days later and asked Steve for a follow-up meeting where he was able to seal the deal with great success.

Sales Tip!

There are no cookie cutter sales techniques that are guaranteed to work every time. If you thoughtfully take your clients' 'pain' points into consideration and are prepared to answer questions about their challenges, then you will be well-positioned for sales success.

If Steve had completed his homework in the initial round, then, after having conversed with his buyer on the phone, he would have arranged a simple presentation that demonstrated the benefits of the line expansion, and he would have immediately provided examples to the buyer to accommodate the change.

Case-in-point: Steve relied on a familiar strategy rather than meeting the client where he was at. When it proved anxiety provoking, he allowed his fears to drive his thought process and his 'pomp and circumstance' sales strategy emerged, clearly alienating his customer.

Turning the Tables

When you go to a doctor, your first question is usually, "What's wrong with me, Doc?" Yet, more often than not, providers won't answer you right away. Instead, they ask you a question in return: "Good question. Where does it hurt?" With this interviewing approach, they elicit more information from you, and you talk more specifically about your 'pain'. The technique of answering a question with a question is called *turning the tables*— otherwise known as Socratic questioning.

When working with your prospects, however, also remember that you have to try and be more of a specialist than a general practitioner. The question that the prospect asks is *never* the real question (Remember the 'Rule of Three'). In order to uncover the underlying problem, the specialist (sales professional) has to move the patient (prospect) through at least two levels of questioning, or turning the tables.

The first question that the prospect asks is usually intellectual in nature. As you turn the tables and use elaborative questioning, however, prospects may think that you don't fully understand the issue at-hand, and they will rephrase the question; usually revealing the real question where it might sound something like this:

Prospect: How is your company different from your competition?
(intellectual question)
You: Good question. What, specifically, do you mean by different? (first turn)
Prospect: Well, how fast does your service department respond?
(intellectual question) **You:** It sounds like fast response is important to you. Is that a fair statement? (second turn)

Prospect: It sure is. I don't want to get stuck with poor service again. **You:** Aha!! you silently mutter.

So why should you turn the tables on a question? Here are

four very good reasons:

1.   To discover the real question behind a particular problem

2.   To stay in control of the interview

3.   To avoid giving the wrong information

4.   To avoid falling into a black hole

The following is an example of the kind of black hole that sales professionals often allow themselves to plunge into:

Prospect: Does this unit print out multiple result sheets?
You: It sure does. You have a choice of 5, 10, 15, or 20 copies at a clip. Which operation would you like to see first?
Prospect: None. I don't want multiple copies.

However, if you employ turning the table skills, then it might sound like this:

 Prospect: Does this unit print out multiple results? (intellectual question) **You**: Good question. Is that important to you? (first turn)
Prospect: I was just wondering if multiple printouts were an option, or if it's automatically built into the unit? (intellectual question) **You:** That's a good point. Can I ask you why it matters? (second turn) **Prospect:** Yes! It's a waste of money. Frankly, I don't want every clerk in my lab making extra copies just in case one happens to be a little off-center. **You:** (Aha!! you silently mutter). That's a very good point. Do you think you would be okay with a copier that had a multiple printout capability but knowing it could only be used with discretion? **Prospect:** Well, yes. That

would make a lot of sense.

Be Gentle, Doctor

No one likes to go to a doctor who treats people with poor bedside manner. Even if he/she is a technical genius, patients won't go if they feel they're not being listened to or are being manhandled.

Sales doctors need to be gentle, too. In this vein, there are two ways to ask questions: abrasively and gently. Your job is to ask a question in response to their questions— with great curiosity and care as each new question responds to your customer's unique challenges and needs. To facilitate, preempt your questions with encouraging phrases such as, "That's a good point," "That makes sense," "Good question," "I'm glad you asked that," "I appreciate you asking me that."

Be Precise

Many of the objections that prospects raise are vague. Try to hone in on sources of resistance right away by memorizing and implementing the following reverse questions:

Prospect: All of these products are alike. **You:** All of them? **Prospect**: This product is too expensive. **You:** Compared to what? **Prospect**: I don't need a lot of bells and whistles. **You**: When you say "bells and whistles," what specifically do you mean?
Prospect: Your presentation doesn't make sense. **You**: How, specifically, doesn't it make sense?
Prospect: I can't make a decision about that today. **You**: Would

you tell me what prevents you from making a decision today?

Flo-with: The Best Way to Handle Resistance

Flo-with is a communication tool for neutralizing resistance while acknowledging a person's divergent point of view. Once a Flo-with statement has been used, it is usually followed by a question that leads the person towards an outcome that supports your original objective.

Utilize this technique to handle resistance from your supervisor, employees, customers, and even with family members. You'll soon see its multiplicative benefits beyond simply disagreeing. How does it work? Flo-with methodology involves agreeing with the other person's statement in order to diffuse the resistance.

Caution: We often tell someone that we agree with them and then insert the word *but* before presenting our own point of view. Using *'but,'* however, negates everything that has been said before it. So eliminate that word from your vocabulary and begin replacing it with Flo-with phrases and techniques.

Follow these three simple steps:

1. Agree.

2. Insert the word "and."

3. Ask another question --one that supports your point of view and which causes your partner to think constructively, along with you, for a solution.

Here are some examples:

Prospect: You just don't understand anything! **You:** You're right, I really don't. What specifically would benefit you if I could understand it?

Or:

Prospect: You don't deliver on your promises. **You:** You're right, we may have made some mistakes in the past. What could we do now to restore your trust?

Or:

Prospect: We just don't have the manpower to take on this project. **You:** What you're saying makes good sense. It's a big job. And how can we work together so we can get the job done?

Try responding to the following challenge statements yourself. It's a good idea to get someone else to practice with you so you can 'flow' (facilitate) each other:

Your presentation skills are just shameful.

The quality of your product is not the best.

Your competitor's product has far more features.

The price is simply too high.

You Don't Have to Be Sick to Get Better

As a sales doctor, your goal is to hook your prospects emotionally as you jointly search for the solution to their concerns and match their needs. Executed well, this client-centered approach creates a sense of urgency while implying that you have a solution that they need to learn about.

Sales Tip!

The master sales professional understands that you must allow prospects to buy rather than be sold to. So pay special attention to these next important steps so that your prospects will schedule your phone calls for you:

You: What is your biggest stumbling block in sales/your telecommunication system/general information tracking *(an area that reveals how use of your product or service would be beneficial)*? We generally find that organizations such as yours will, at one time or another, experience difficulty in the area of employee motivation and performance/obtaining new business and profitability/time management/inventory control *(just identify three areas where your product or service helps to solve* their *problems)*. Can you help me?
Prospect: *(The prospect will tell you.)* **You:** Can you tell me more? How did you prioritize your needs? *(probing further in order to get them to amplify their first answer)*
Or, **You:** When you say . . ., help me understand it more. What exactly do you mean by that? Or, *(the best question in the world)* **You:** Oh? *(The prospect has no choice but to go on and tell you more!)*
If the prospect insists that nothing is wrong or in need of change, say: **You:** So, you mean everything is going well, and nothing can stand improvement?

If the resistance continues, offer: **You:** When you think about the last time you used (whatever your product or service is), are there any issues or concerns that come to mind? Are there any areas in which you could use improvement? (Make a joke, since you know that you don't have to get sick to get better!)

Making It Hurt

Think about it: If you went to the doctor for a routine check-up, and your provider found something wrong, then you'd probably feel concerned. Depending on the problem, you might also be ready to do almost anything to find a cure. So, again, play the role of the doctor:

You: What is this problem costing you in terms of reputation, time, or money? In round numbers, how much would that amount to in, say, a year?
You: What have you done to fix this problem? **Prospect:** *(They will tell you what they've tried.)* **You:** And that worked well for you?

No matter what, you know that their current system hasn't worked, because they already admitted that they still have the problem. By prompting their memory and asking them to list all of the things that haven't *worked*, you involve them emotionally. They'll start to feel the 'pain' and, more and more, they'll be craving a solution.

You: This is all very interesting, but, tell me this, are you committed to solving this problem? Or, **You:** Are you committed to correcting this situation in the future?

This is the critical close. Once this question has been answered with an affirmative "yes," then you can be certain that you are on your way to a dedicated sale.

If, however, prospects indicate that they are interested

rather than committed, then suggest, over the years, you have learned that *interested* people generally have minimal needs, a tighter budget, or, perhaps, are just beginning to comparison shop. In contrast, customers who have a *commitment* are ready and willing to make decisions, taking action to correct or enhance company performance, productivity, or profitability.

The following is a list of some of the best questions that you can and should ask a potential buyer at any time:

1.   When you say . . ., what do you mean by that? *(Be sure to repeat any descriptive word or phrase that your prospect uses such as "infrequently," "some difficulty," or "top priority.")*

2. That's a very good question. Can you help me understand more?

3. You mean, you never have any problems? And, things always go right, too? *(Note: About the only time that you ever want to use absolutes in the sales process is when you're repeating a prospect's words and using them in the form of a question.*

4.   Oh? *(Remember, this simple statement is very supportive and, with its inherent emotional appeal, it immediately encourages them to expound on whatever they just said.)*

5.   Can you be more specific? What prompted you to ask that?

6.   Can you tell me why that's a priority for you?

7.   Take a minute, and let's imagine that I just said 'yes'

or 'no'— what difference would that make to you?

Qualifying Exam

1.   What's your primary concern with (insert your line of work)?

2.   How long have you been wrestling with this issue?

3.   What is this problem costing you in terms of time, productivity, funds, and credibility?

4.   What have you done to fix it?

5.   And that's worked well for you?

6.   Do you have a (feasible) budget set up to solve this problem?

7.   Are you the person who makes these decisions?

8.   Are you committed to finding a solution to this problem?

Chapter 4/ Step 3 Summary

1.   Locate the source/s of the customer's 'pain' by asking open-ended questions.

2.   Qualify the prospect.

3.   Make your presentation. But, *never* before the first two steps have been accomplished.

Sales Tip!

Do *not* answer questions that haven't been asked or offer solutions to problems that may not exist (making your interaction unnecessarily complex or going into unchartered, dangerous territory). Remember: Less is always more, and you won't need to recover from any errors!

Instead, support an open flow of information/communication by responding to a question with another question (turning the tables and demonstrating genuine interest). Also, soften your questions so they don't sound like a challenge.

Why?

☆ To discover the real (underlying) question or problem

☆ To avoid giving the wrong information and, worse, falling into a black hole

☆ To maintain control of the interview

Be gentle, precise, and, when met with any resistance, implement the three steps of *Flo-with:*

1.   Agree.

2.   Replace the word *but* with and.

3.   Ask another question to clarify your prospect's needs and to gradually reframe your perspective and its benefits.

When you've found the 'pain', make sure that the prospect is not only aware of the symptoms but also of the short-and long-term effects and the need for change.

Chapter 5 - Step 4: Budget, Terms and Conditions

Discovering the Budget

Remember, a qualified prospect has three attributes:

1.   A concern and need—which you've already established through careful questioning methodology as a 'sales doctor.'

2.   A budget

3.   A decision maker

Once you have diagnosed the prospects' 'pain', you must establish whether they have 'health insurance,' so to speak. That is, do they have the budget to finance your recommended treatment?

In Step 3, your buyer became emotionally involved in pursuit of a cure. Now, your objective is to discuss budgets while involvement is high and the prospect is acutely aware of how much your intervention is worth.

Typically, clients don't divulge their financial information with you, but it is important to discuss funding in a transparent manner before investing your time and energy into a demo or, certainly, a well-prepared presentation.

Sales Tip!

Don't make presentations to *unqualified* prospects. This step only spends valuable energy, time, and money. Review the problems that the prospects have revealed and ask more questions, such as: "What kind of budget do you have for solving these issues?"

If they don't want to openly disclose, then you probably haven't established sufficient rapport or exposed the severity or intensity of their 'pain.' Therefore, you might want to be a little more specific as you test the waters:

You: "In another office like yours, I imagine it costs about $1,000 a month to deal with similar problems."

Either of these methods draws the prospects' cards on the table, and the response will surely indicate whether or not you should continue with your interview.

Sometimes, you gain more unusual responses like, "Money is no object," and you can bet on one of three outcomes:

1.   Money is no object, because they don't have any to begin with!

2.   The buck stops here as you are not talking to the decision maker.

3.   *You* are facing the competition.

The following exchange illustrates how to graciously discover the budget:

You: And tell me, do you have a budget set aside to help correct this problem?

Prospect: Yes.

You: Well, would you mind sharing it with me? **Prospect:** (They usually do mind.) **You:** Can you tell me in round numbers so I can know if we're in the same ballpark? *(Work with them and be patient here as budgets are a private matter.)* **Prospect:** Pausing. **You:** Well, would you estimate it's more than $5,000 and less than $10,000? And, closer to

$5,000 or closer to $10,000?

Keep narrowing it down, getting as close as you can. At the very least, just establish that they have a negotiable budget, and, at that point, you can discuss it more as the process continues.

Prospect: I really have no idea. I've never done this before. **You**: Okay. I understand that. So, let's envision it's the *(day of the job, end of the job, you just got the delivery, whatever),* and you've just received the bill. You peer down to read it. What does it say? What do you see? *(Here, tap into your new knowledge of neuro-linguistics to help mirror and match their processing and communicative style.)*

Or, **Prospect:** No, at this time, we don't have any designated budget, because the money is out. **You:** Okay, and how were you hoping that I could help you? Or, **You:** Well, have you set aside a specific budget for this particular product/service? **Prospect:** How much does it cost? **You:** Well, we always work to cater to both your business and budgeting needs so our solutions range from around $3,000 to $18,000.

Which end of the spectrum would you say you are closer to in your ability to finance a solution to your problem? **Prospect:** Closer to $3,000. **You:** Can you tell me in round numbers how close? **Prospect:** About $4,000.

At this point, if prospects affirm that they really don't have a budget right now, then ask them to disclose when they likely will. If that approach doesn't elicit a timetable that you consider reasonable, then it may be time to 'go for no'— that is, to *abort* the sales interview.

Never be afraid to go for 'no.' If you aren't going to be able to arrange a package that is mutually satisfying to both sides, then you're better off discovering that in ten minutes rather than after three hours of work.

Remember: *'No'* is the second-best answer that you can get. The best, of course, is *'yes.'* But, the answer you don't want, the one that is not only rather infuriating but also unacceptable is, "I'll think it over. Maybe...," or "I'll get back to you" as their evident indecision leaves both of you in-limbo. Urge the prospect to decide between 'yes' and 'no,' with 'no' being *perfectly okay* with you.

In order to finish qualifying your prospect and to reinforce what you are prepared to do, we have developed a technique for your use. Say to the prospect: "We've found that companies such as yours (or individuals like yourself) generally fall into one of four categories:

1.   They are very interested in our product or service, and they have a set budget.

2.   They are very interested in our product or service, and they don't have a budget.

3.   They have no interest in our product or service, but they have a budget.

4.   They have no interest in our product or service, and they don't have a budget.

"Can you help me? Which category describes your situation best?" Depending on their response, you should ask the appropriate matching question below:

1.   What specifically were you hoping we could do for you?

2.   And what were you hoping we could do for you without a budget?

3.   Is there anything you would like to change or improve?

4.   I'm wondering if I can help you with anything?

If the prospects indicate they are in category one, then they are *hot* prospects. If they are in categories two or three, then they are *warm* or *cool,* depending on whether or not they are the decision makers. If they are in the fourth category, then, evidently, they are *cold* prospects, and you should just let this situation go.

If the prospects answer your exploratory comment about cost with, "That's a lot of money," then you can respond with, "Oh, OK. Can you help me? Relative to what?" and wait . . .
Depending on their answer, you may have to ask your customers to suggest a number that they consider workable. If the figure they suggest is too low, then it's up to you to maintain control and to assess (1) if their figure represents an actual quote from another supplier and (2) whether you want to —or have to— either quickly match the competition for strategic purposes or just end the sales interview.

But beware: This situation shouldn't happen if you've established close rapport and posed the kinds of questions that would expose the buyers' 'pain.'

Put Your Cards on the Table

Along with the budget, you have to establish other critical terms and conditions such as credit applications, deposits, retainers, payments, payment plans, and time frame for implementation. It is essential to discuss the available options upfront so that both parties are prepared for each others' negotiation.

If you confront a problem when attempting to finalize a decision, then don't shirk away in order to avoid rejection. Face it boldly, head on. Respond with, "We have a problem here." Let the prospects say, "What is it?" and work collaboratively to establish a solution.

If they can't, then it's time to say, "Well, it's been helpful to get to know you, and it sounds as if our conversation is over." If they return with, "Wait a minute . . .," obviously their 'pain' is rather intense, they need your cure, and the deal will soon be sealed.

If the prospects' answer reveals that you are too far apart to reach an agreement, however, then this juncture could also signal that it's time to go for 'no.' If the situation is clearly hopeless, you can always level, "Off the record, before we hang up, what's the real reason you aren't going to be able to use our product (or service)?

Listen carefully to their answer as you might learn something very valuable that you can use next time (with another, more flexible client or company). Or, if you're fortunate enough, then you may finally deduce the real reason and continue to sell armed with this knowledge.

Asking your prospects to qualify themselves is really the best way to establish a mutually understood upfront expectation. When you treat the specifics of the business transaction with openness and sincerity, prospects tend to be more serious and honest with you. Since most clients respect business professionals who put their cards on the table straight from the beginning, why wait any longer?

Chapter 5/ Step 4 Summary

There are three requisites for qualifying a prospect:

1. Find a need.

2. Find a budget.

3. Find the decision maker.

Don't spend your resources making presentations to unqualified prospects! Don't be afraid to 'go for no' as appropriate, and remember that 'no' is the second best response that you can hope for. It frees you to follow your plan so that you can obtain the 'yes' that you truly want and deserve for all of your enthusiasm and diligent work.

Chapter 6 – Step 5: Finding the Decision Maker

After you discover your buyers' need and sales budget, there is still one more requirement to qualify your prospect. You must ascertain that you are consulting with the correct person; the one who yields the power to make executive decisions.

As described, many of today's sales professionals start by knowing very little about their prospects. They make calls to individuals who reside at very low levels of management, and they usually remain with these non-decision-makers, reaping minimal, if any, success.

If you are at this level, then it can be a very painful experience to wade through the hierarchy in order to graduate to the decision-making plane. You might even find yourself feeling stonewalled, threatened, or, worse, blackballed as you mustn't cross boundaries by attempting to rise above your contact's head.

However, there are tools that you can use to ensure that you reach the proper contact at the beginning of your relationship. Most prospects indicate that they are the decision maker, but it is important to qualify this assertion without being offensive. In the area of decision-making, you have to determine who, besides the person you're speaking with, has to be involved and how, when, and why this is the policy.

With regard to committee or group decisions, your mission is to obtain the names, titles, roles, and functions of each member and to request a phone consultation with each of them for interviewing purposes.

In any business or organization, there is a chain of command. As sales representatives, your job is to start with the primary decision maker. If your research is done correctly and you have identified the corporate officer, CEO, owner, or other head administrator, then your first and primary level of contact has already been located. *Always start here.*

Sales Tip!

When trying to discover the decision maker, begin from the top and gradually, methodically move down the hierarchy.

Eighty percent of the time, you will reach the most knowledgeable person in the company on the line— the personal assistant to the top officer. That's the person who you really want to interview and to ask for help. Your next step will be connecting with the chief corporate officer. Before calling, you might use e-mailing to introduce yourself and your product. A few days after your introduction, call the person directly for an interview:

You: Hi, I'm Bob Doe from XYZ Company. I hope you had an opportunity to review the information I recently sent you. Oh, you have . . . Well, that's great! In that case, I'd like to arrange a convenient time for a phone consultation so that we can exchange ideas concerning the information you received and see how we can best help each other.
Prospect: What day are you looking at? *(No matter what*

the prospect says, respond with:) **You:** I'm sorry, that's a really hard day for me to schedule— I'm booked. Can you please find another day? **Prospect:** *(Whatever they say).* **You:** Good. What time? Can we make that at 3:10pm? *(Or 10:40am, etc.; you'll look busier if you select a time that's slightly atypical.)*

At this point in the selling cycle, one of three scenarios will inevitably occur: The chief operating officer may talk to you, you'll be introduced to someone else, or, for whatever reason, your efforts will be stalled. In this case, just take a deep breath, and move on to more fruitful prospects.

If the chief officer will talk with you, one of two situations will result from your conversation. You will either deal entirely with the primary officer, or the primary officer will want to introduce you to someone else after your initial presentation. If this person is the one whom you will deal with throughout the selling cycle, then just continue with your sales approach.

However, if the primary contact wishes to introduce you to someone else after your initial call, then be flexible. Remember this rule-of-thumb: It is always better to be 'passed down' the corporate ladder than to be 'passed up' by an initial purchasing agent and sideswiped from the rungs altogether.

Ask the chief officer to introduce you as this personal touch gives you more credibility at the next level of contact. If this option is not possible, then simply inform the new point person that you are calling at the CEO's suggestion.

Additionally, let all contacts know that you will keep their office aware about future developments.

From here, be ready that your new contact will either continue with you directly or introduce you to another follow-up lead. Your job is to determine who provides the final approval and, therefore, has the authority to authorize the purchase or placement. You need to work with them, whether directly or indirectly, and be certain that you maintain open communication with the other levels.

Who's Who in Decision-Making?

Let's identify the typical levels of contact as well as their basic functions and decision-making authority.

PURCHASING/OFFICE SERVICES

The purchasing/office services personnel are usually concerned with hardware, machine specifications, general costs, and maintaining the status quo. Unless higher-level management complains about specific equipment, their attitude is usually 'don't make waves.' So, depending on the company, these individuals display a wide range of authority.

MIDDLE MANAGEMENT

Middle management is usually responsible for developing and implementing programs to fulfill corporate goals and objectives. Because their level of authority is usually higher, they could represent valuable input sources that influence final decisions.

SENIOR MANAGEMENT

Senior management officers are usually concerned with the company's 'big picture' goals and determine fiscal accountability as they answer to stockholders or taxpayers.

In most cases, higher management prefers a systematic and organized approach to managing their operations. For example, many companies have programs with other organizations that provide them with discounts for multiple purchases. These contracts offer quality products at a lower cost.

Perhaps, this type of negotiation is something that you can offer a new client or customer. Remember: When an account has already accepted the concept associated with your program or product, most of your selling obstacles are already behind you.

A final purchasing agent will not necessarily think along these lines, however. In these cases, senior management is concerned with factors like general operation costs, productivity, inflation, and energy conservation. In major commercial accounts, these variables affect the bottom line, and, in government accounts, controlling these costs ensures the best possible value for every tax dollar spent.

Executives at this level are also preoccupied with long-range results and ways to flourish. They have to plan for programs and systems that assist them so, if you can match their needs, then it's likely that you can also grow with them.

Essentially, managers want to implement better ways to

lead their business, and, to be successful, it's your responsibility to identify the most relevant and state-of-the-art intervention. Conversely, purchasing agents do not look for change unless senior management urges them and, while concerned with a good return on their investment, senior staff are not necessarily sold on the lowest bid. Thank goodness for you!

Examples of Contact Levels for Senior Management

Medical
Resident Chief Physicians
Hospital Administrators
Lab Technicians
Pathologists
Purchasing Managers

Commercial
Chairperson of the Board, President Executive, Vice President, Vice President for Administration, Vice President of Finance, Divisional Vice President

Government, City
Mayor, City Manager, Assistant to Mayor

Government, County
County Commissioners, County Managers

Government, State
Governor Lieutenant, Governor Comptroller, Agency Heads Department, Secretary

Government, Federal—Civilian
Department Heads, Agency Directors

Government, Federal—Military
Commanding Officers, Executive Officers

Education District
Superintendent, Curriculum Director, Assistant Superintendent, Business Manager

Colleges/Universities
Chancellor, Provost, Vice Provost, President, Vice President, Dean, Department Head

More Tips for Pinpointing the Decision Maker

Of course, you'll need solid navigating skills to help you distinguish the real decision makers from the self-appointed ones after grasping their true budget:

You: Let's assume that I can offer you a solution to this problem at a price we can agree on. Would you be the person who makes these decisions?
Prospect: Yes. **You:** Does that mean that you don't need anyone else's approval? **Prospect:** Yes. Or, **Prospect:** No. There's a board that I have to present a proposal to, and the members make the ultimate decision. **You:** At some point, would it be helpful for me to talk with the members to present the *(program, idea, product)* more comprehensively? **Prospect:** No. Those decisions are made by *(so and so)*. **You:** Great to know. In that case, can you help me connect with them? *(If no:)* Well, then, can you help me reach *(so and so)*, and may I use your name when I speak to them? *(Again, always try to turn the call into a referred lead.)*

At this point in the sales process, eliminate diluted 'think-it-over' and 'maybe' responses, and go for a solid decision. As needed, also realize when "I'll think it over" responses *are* decisions *not* to make a decision to avoid grasping onto fading and false hope:

You: Assuming that we can deliver a solution that satisfies your needs *(list their 'pains' in order of priority),* and we can do that within your budget, when do you foresee a more reliable *(or faster, easier, etc.)* system in use here?
Prospect: Well, as soon as possible. **You:** Great, and are you able to make the yes or no decision regarding this *(product or service),* or will you need to talk it over with anyone else in your organization? **Prospect:** I may discuss it with my office manager, but I make the final decision.

You: Will you be able to make a yes or no decision at the time of the demonstration, with 'yes' or 'no' both being perfectly acceptable responses? **Prospect:** Yes. Or, **You:** Will you be able to make a yes or no decision at the time of the presentation, with both being perfectly acceptable responses? **Prospect:** No. **You:** Would you be willing to tell me why? **Prospect:** Yes, I have to shop around. I have three other vendors to consult with before I make a decision. **You:** I see. Could I ask you a hypothetical question? **Prospect:** Sure. **You:** Let's imagine for a minute that, after seeing our system, you like it so much that you decide you don't want to spend your precious time looking at other products. What would I have to provide you with today so that you could make that kind of time-saving decision?

Take notes, folks, because they're telling you what you need to do in order to sell them at the presentation. Or, **You:** Will you be able to make a yes or no decision at the time of my presentation, with both being perfectly acceptable? **Prospect:** No. **You:** Would you be willing to tell me why? **Prospect:** Yes. I have to shop around. I have three other vendors to consult with before I make a decision. **You:** Oh. I see. And, off the record, what would it really take for us to do business?

Again, listen carefully. By taking consumers 'off the record,' they have an opportunity to open up uncensored.

Chapter 6/ Step 5 Summary

1.   When trying to identify the decision maker, start from the top of the organization and work down.

2.   Keep track of everyone you talk to and find out where they fit into the 'big picture.'

3.   Be sure to get personal introductions whenever possible.

4.   Keep each person you've been introduced to up-to-date on your progress.

5.   If you have developed a special rapport with someone inside a company, try to enlist that person as a guide. An inside 'shepherd' cannot only help you to navigate your way but can also share valuable feedback regarding others' reactions to your approaches.

Chapter 7 - Step 6: The Review

You have now reached the end of the first half of the sales process. It is time to review what has transpired so far.

Review Tip #1

Be certain that you have developed rapport with the prospect. Having rapport means that you have established credibility and trust and that the prospect is now comfortable enough to answer your questions *truthfully*. You can then investigate so-called 'pain symptoms' (problem areas in need of remediation) by probing with further questions.

Review Tip #2

You've uncovered or established a ballpark budget, conversed with the decision maker and their advisers, identified your competition, and already scheduled a follow-up appointment for your prospect to review your transaction and to make decisions.

Review Tip #3

Go over your notes with the prospect. Arrive at an agreement about what transpired during the day's transaction and what you would like to occur the next time that you talk. Try following up with something like:

Today, we decided that you have the following issues and concerns *(prioritize them; you should have at least five)*. When you've tested the samples and we regroup next week,

I'll share with you how we can help solve these problems within the budget that you've provided. Then, at the time, can you agree to make a decision as to whether or not you would like to go ahead with our product or service, with both 'yes' or 'no' being perfectly acceptable responses? Does that sound fair to you?

Convince your customer to agree to make a decision after your next conversation, whether 'yes' or 'no.' If you're aware that they must submit your proposal to a board or committee after they review it, then try to schedule an appointment with the board members yourself. Bear in mind that, since a board is composed of many individuals, they have to be sold separately— yes, that's right, *one at a time.*

Sales Tip!

Make sure that you don't end your interview without making an appointment for a follow-up meeting. This saves you both time and energy while establishing a platform for rapport.

If customers have to see your presentation before arranging with the board, then persuade them to agree that they will, at least, make a decision regarding submitting your product or service to the board at the next opportunity. This agreement is called an *upfront contract.* As noted, be certain that you don't end your interview without making a follow-up appointment.

The Second Interview

Review your upfront contract from the first interview, paying special attention to rapport. Tell the prospect:

Last week, we agreed that, if I can show you how we can solve the problems you listed to your satisfaction and at a price within your budget, then you would make a 'yes' or 'no' decision today, with 'no' being perfectly acceptable. Is that a fair statement?

Then review the target problems, asking for any feedback. Read the list carefully, and remember: You should have identified about five concerns. If you don't have five areas, then the close may be less powerful as you'll see in Chapter 10.

Chapter 7/ Step 6 Summary

1.   Make sure that you have solid rapport with the prospect.

2.   Once having agreed upon a ballpark budget, establishing the decision maker and relevant advisers, know your competition, and make a follow-up appointment.

3.   Jointly review your notes, come to an agreement about the nature of the day's transaction, and establish an agenda for the next time that you meet.

4. Persuade the prospect to make a decision regarding the submission of your product or service to the board at the next opportunity; your *upfront contract.*

5. Make sure that you don't end your interview without

making a follow-up appointment.

Chapter 8 – Step 7: The Presentation

If steps 1 through 6 of the sales interview process have been thoroughly completed, then this next step will flow easily, with the prospect actively participating in your presentation. In fact, *this is not the time* to be lecturing to a silent audience. You have, ideally, listed five, or, at least, a minimum of three, of your prospect's problems and are now ready for action.

Ask your customer to highlight the most important problem for you to solve first. Review your approach and seek confirmation that the issue can now be eliminated.

Do not move on until the prospect is satisfied. As you attempt to address each concern in priority order, be sure to ask if each one is resolved 100 %. If not, review the problem and your solution again until reaching this level of satisfaction, and then cross the problem off the prospect's list.

Sales Tip!

Warning: Never, *ever* begin a sales interview with your presentation.

Aim to resolve at least two out of three or three out of the five problems that you have jointly identified. Also, be sure that *you don't do* a complete presentation, since you want to keep your prospects hooked to the point that they will close on the product or service themselves.

During your presentation, *primary video-oriented individuals* will need to picture your presentation, *primary audio-oriented customers will need* to hear and interact, and *primary kino-oriented prospects* will need to sense and to experience your presentation through experimenting with demos and materials.

Using a sample test kit, *video-oriented individuals* pay more attention to how the kit is organized as well as accompanying brochures and materials that they can scan. *Audio-oriented clients* are more impressed by your descriptions and invest a great deal into others' testimonials at various levels in the company hierarchy. Finally, *kino-oriented consumers* need a hands-on experience; again, to explore 'the feel of it.'

Again, don't let success at *any* stage of your presentation lead you to believe that it's time to cast a pitch for something that is new. Only address the needs that your prospect has discussed and that you have both agreed to target.

Chapter 8/ Step 7 Summary

1.   You should not be lecturing to a silent audience.

2.   After having listed three to five of your prospect's problems, ask the customer to isolate the most important issue for you to solve first.

3.   Do not go on to the next concern until the prospect is fully satisfied.

4.   Be sure to resolve two out of three or three out of the five problems jointly listed.

5.   And, whatever you do, *don't complete* the

presentation!

Chapter 9 – Step 8: The Reinforcement

At this stage, it is important to know where you stand so take the prospect's temperature. After solving three of the problems 100 %, tell your customer:

You: We've addressed some of the issues that are important to you. I know that we have other issues to discuss, but, to get some feedback on where we are in the process, can you help me? On a scale from 0 to 10, with 0 being that you are not at all interested in our product or service and 10 being that you can already see it as a valuable addition to your business, where do you see/hear/feel us being now? As described, access your new knowledge of neuro-linguistics to customize this question and to make it even more robust.

If the prospect is at a 6 or above, then ask what you must do to arrive closer to, if not to reach a 10. If you can satisfy the prospect's request, do it and then check their pulse again.

If the prospect is at 5 or below, then recognize that you have an emergency. In fact, it means that you did not fully qualify and uncover the 'pain'. Try:

You: With such a low number, can you help me to help you? What did I say or do or not say or do during my presentation to earn such a low rating? What do we need to review that I misunderstood or overlooked before we can move forward?

Continue to question and probe until you discover what exactly went wrong so that you can correct it to the best of your ability. If the prospect has not reached 10 before you finish demonstrating, however, you must finish the presentation and proceed to your summary.

Summarize the 'pains' that have been relieved and the buying criteria that have been satisfied, gaining the prospect's agreement as you go. Afterwards, ask if there are any questions. If there are, probe to ascertain what specifically would be needed to approach a 10.

When the prospect reaches 10-- Stop right away! Again, the prospect has 'self-closed' so *do not solve* the other problems. In layman's terms, to go any farther is called 'talking yourself out of a sale.' Instead, ask the prospect, "What would you like me to do now?"

When this step has been completed, it is finally time to go for the close-- swiftly but softly.

Chapter 9/ Step 8 Summary

1.   Here, in the reinforcement step, is where you check the prospect's temperature/pulse.

2.   After solving at least three of your customer's problems, ask him/her to evaluate their interest in your product or service on a scale from 0 to 10; that is from no interest to fully satisfied.

Be sure to customize your question utilizing your client's primary representational system.

Chapter 10 – Step 9 The Close

Closing the sale is the end result of all of your previous work: If you have properly uncovered the 'pain' and qualified your client, established the budget, agreed upon the decision to be made and by whom, and proved yourself and product in a dynamic presentation, then the close will be easy.

Because you check the prospect's temperature during the presentation, you will also know when to close— that is, when you get to 10! Specifically, after you solve the fourth problem identified, ask the prospect where he or she stands. Then, ask again what the prospect would like to do. The usual response is to solve the final problem. At this point, the prospect typically recognizes a win-win situation and enjoys actively participating in the close.

When you reach 10, you must follow-up with, "What do we need to do now with regard to the purchase order and delivery?" Although the sale isn't officially closed until you reach a 10, your prospect may give you a buying signal along the way. This signal can be defined as a verbal or an audible sign that indicates your prospect is beginning to see, hear, or feel him/herself attaching to your product or service.

However, a buying signal is not necessarily a sign that the prospect is ready to close either, so stick to your plan and don't 'jump the gun.' Recognize that a buying signal is really an opportunity for you to cement the value of your product or service, and you can accomplish this measure by encouraging your prospect to discuss his/her experience using your product or service.

Here are some buying signals and the appropriate

responses:

Prospect: That's fantastic! **You:** What's the most fantastic thing about it? Or, **Prospect:** I really like that feature. **You:** What specifically is it that you like? Or, **Prospect:** When could I have delivery? **You:** When would you prefer delivery? Or, **Prospect:** What about follow-up service? **You:** Good question. What specific area would you like me to address?

Physical buying signals might include the following:

☆The prospect suddenly takes a deep breath and relaxes.

☆The prospect has a 'smile' in his or her voice (using a very affirmative tone).

☆The prospect suddenly becomes friendlier.

☆The prospect discusses ordering details.

☆The prospect makes numerical calculations.

When you question a buying signal, you help clients to finalize details or to conceptualize global strengths so that, ultimately, they may convince and close the deal themselves.

Sales Tip!

If you can remember to match your prospect's vocabulary, tone, and physiology when questioning, you will be building your close with even more powerful tools. Even at this point, you don't want to contaminate rapport by overselling or requesting an order prematurely. Instead, continue mirroring and decide if this moment is the correct time to take the prospect's temperature.

The minute that your prospect alerts you that you're at 10, stop! When the customer confirms being at 10, that prospect is sold. Gently remind the client of the agreement to make a 'yes' or a 'no' decision, and wait, just wait. Not even a word! Even if the silence feels very uncomfortable, remember that you are in control.

At this point, if you are working with someone who still has to gain a board or committee approval, then encourage the person to allow you to present your product or service to the board committee,— one-by-one to persuade them that you can best represent your product and match their needs.

Remember— there are *no magic closes*. No telemarketer can rescue a mishandled sale, and the sales professional earns a strong close by establishing the nature and severity of the prospect's 'pain', the budget, and the 'who's-who' in decision-making ability. The sales professional then demonstrates how to alleviate the sources of 'pain' and, by tapping both emotional appeal and rationale problem solving, a customer will deduce how a product or service can make a very valuable impact on daily operations and functioning.

A thorough qualification of the prospect is also vital to a successful close. So remember that closing begins with your first contact with the prospect, your genuine interest in your consumer's needs, and your ability to foster a positive image of yourself, your product, and your company.

Chapter 10/ Step 9 Summary

Remember: Closing the sale stems from accumulated work. Although laborious, you will feel as satisfied as your customers if you have: uncovered the 'pain', established a budget, arrived at a joint decision, and cultivated a positive image, especially during your presentation.

Chapter 11 – Step 10: After The Sale

After you have entered your final sales order and confirmed it with your client, then probe your prospect's understanding of its broader implications.

They usually respond by saying that it's a contract. "Yes," you can clarify, "and it's the beginning of my commitment to working with you. How does that seems/sound/feel for you?"

If they're not completely satisfied, then review whatever elements still induce apprehension or discomfort. If they are comfortable, however, then you have just reinforced the sale and enhanced feelings of trust and loyalty with your new clients.

The follow-up and follow-through calls are proof of your commitment to an ongoing relationship. So, don't make the mistake of waiting until there's a question or a problem to resolve to touch base again. Alternatively, call with care and enthusiasm and assert, "I wanted to verify that our delivery was prompt and that the correct material arrived without any problems."

Sales Tip!

Become an accessible and active resource that your clients will use, appreciate, and rely on again-and-again; that is, understand the difference between *serving your clients* and merely *servicing them.*

These points of contact also bolster your after-market and referral business. No one wants to start the selling cycle all over again, time after time. Yet, many sales professionals operate in this fashion and end up working much more than they actually need to.

Eighty percent of your business comes from twenty percent of your client introductions. So, every time that you make a sale, ask for a referral. Write the contact information down along with the name of the customer who passed it to you and other key details learned from your conversations.

Each time that you make a sale from a referral, be sure to send a personalized and hand-written thank you note (rather than an email) to the customer who provided the lead. Always remember the value of your client; treat him/her as Confucius would recommend to continue in a relationship where the rewards will begin to multiply.

Realize that successful business in the 21st century translates into sellers, buyers, and other administrators banding together through effective needs assessment and reliable delivery. Every client, no matter how small, is a valuable one. Being a master sales professional demands constant, clear communication; patience; and reinforcement of both others and yourself.

So, give yourself permission to enjoy the business and lifestyle that you have worked diligently and artfully to create. If nurtured and maintained properly, it will bring you financial security as well as personal freedom and fulfillment knowing that you have mastered the art of creative problem solving in a competitive market.

Be proud of yourself. You have taken the first critical steps (of many) to accomplishing your goals. The most challenging part is beginning, and you are already set on your path.

Sample Review Questions for the Step-by-Step Sales Interview

Now, it's time to challenge yourself by answering the following questions. If you need any help, just go back and re-read relevant sections. Certainly, the better you know the material presented, then the more successful you will be when conducting your own sales interviews. So, remember to practice, practice, practice!

1.   What should you do each time you speak with a prospect?

2.   What are the primary sensory channels that people use when communicating and that you should always mirror during a sales contact? (Be sure to list words/phrases used by each type).

3.   Define the importance of rapport.

4.   As a sales professional what is the first step that you need to take?

5.   What technique can you use for establishing a customer's budget?

6.   Describe the purpose of using reverse questioning and then reverse the following as asked by a prospect: "Is your product very expensive?"

7.   What does "Money is no object" really mean?

8.   Explain the three steps of *Flo-with* and provide an

example.

9.   What are the three chief factors that you need to know in order to (truly) qualify a prospect?

10.   Which level of management should you approach about your product or service?

11.   How can you transform being introduced 'down' a corporate chain into a 'referred' lead?

12.   Describe an upfront contract.

13.   Approximately how many problems should be on your review list?

14.   What should you do if a prospect refuses to go any further?

15.   How do you deal with a decision-making committee or a board?

16.   How can the science of neuro-linguistics ensure that your presentation flows easily?

17. What should you do if a problem is not solved to your prospect's satisfaction?

18. When does closing begin?

19. Describe the function and utility of buying signals.

20. What should you do every time you make a sale?

Chapter 12: Why Sales Careers Plateau

Generally speaking, careers don't just burn out— *people burn out!* And, if you're finding yourself unmotivated or depressed because of a so-called plateaued sales career, well, then look again--very likely, the plateau may reflect something about you.

Reason #1: Resistance to Change

It's no secret: Business is rapidly changing, and, as a modern sales professional, you are faced with more decisions than ever before. In fact, during your lifetime, it is predicted that you will face 10 or 15 major change-related decisions; many related to and shaping your career landscape. Developing strategies for effectively managing change is one of the most important steps to preventing plateaus and/or to transforming them into opportunities for growth throughout your professional selling career.

How To Deal With Change

There are three main ways that people and organizations change:

Shock: 60 % of change— Reacting to an event that is sudden and painful such as illness or downsizing, which likely creates a physical and psychological response.

Evolution: 20 % of change— Staying inert and avoiding change so that, when it actually occurs around you, any possible response is, more often than not, 'too little too late.'

Choice: 20 % of change- This is where you want to be!

These individuals are very versatile and, although challenging, make routine efforts to adapt to needed changes. They stay apace with business and technology and exude resilience.

The Four Rules of Effective Change

Rule #1: No one can change you, and you can't change anyone else. You must admit your need, stop engaging in denial, and accept responsibility for changing yourself.

Rule #2: Habits aren't necessarily broken, but rather they are replaced by layering new behavior patterns on top of old, familiar ones. Unless extremely dedicated to change, this process usually takes several months to a year. Some motivational speakers assert that a person can learn a new habit in 21 days. We disagree as it can take you that long just to learn much less begin to apply the motions of a new skill.

Don't expect immediate results from whatever program you install in your company, institution, or home. Give it a year and stick with it, knowing that your new way, despite stumbling blocks, can actually last a lifetime; in some cases, with matching effects.

Rule #3: Adhered to over time, a daily routine will become automatic; like procedural memory. But, if you want to become successful, then begin by working with others who are successful.

Rule #4: Having changed a habit, avoid common triggers to effectively lead both yourself and others; whether prospects or colleagues.

Reason #2: Relying Too Much on Your Own Wisdom

No matter how intelligent a company president may be, that officer still relies on a team (otherwise known as a *board of directors*) to steer the organization in the most advantageous, profitable directions. So, how is this fact related to your ability to launch and to maintain a successful sales career? Well, just as most large companies acknowledge the importance of a qualified board of directors, many successful sales professionals have opted for their own personal board of directors to help them navigate their careers.

Think of a personal board as your 'inner circle'; each person holds privileged information about your personal and professional life. Choose your mentors wisely as they can become life guides. Of course, you can always make changes, but a true richness flows from working together during positive and negative experiences inherent to the long haul.

Getting Started: Developing Your Personal Board of Directors

Let's begin with the obvious. Your personal board might include a physician as a health/medical resource, a banker for financial guidance, a CPA for tax input, an attorney for legal advice, and another leader who might provide significant alternative support. Here are some of the less but equally important choices: a business owner in your industry (just not a competitor, please!), a sales and marketing professional, a public relations expert, a business coach, a human resource professional, a webmaster for technical support, and an executive in a dissimilar industry for perspective-taking.

Working With Your Board

Once you have formed your personal board, the next step is to brainstorm a list of ways that your board can support your success. Examples of topics to discuss might include early career development, later advancement in your company, starting a business, how to handle challenging employees or suppliers, financial planning, the relocation of your family for professional or personal reasons, and nurturing the health of your marriage. You see, your board members can be a very rich resource in diverse ways as long as you speak openly, honestly, and are open to their feedback (no matter the input).

Sales Tip!

While your board can provide you with powerful guidance, remember that the final decision must always be yours. When making these critical decisions, always consider a pros-cons analysis before eliciting feedback and store this summary sheet for future use. Finally, enhance the clarity of your decisions by contracting with yourself and agreeing to re-evaluate your results at a later point marked in your agenda.

Communicating With Your Board

The next step is to decide how often to consult with your board. For some, monthly may be perfect while, for others, twice a year is sufficient. The frequency is up to you and your board members, but it should depend on the magnitude, momentum, and impact of decisions that you are making.

Here are some examples of ways that you can communicate with your board: in person, by video chat, teleconference, or phone, e-mail, fax, or letter. With today's wide range of technology, the distance between you and your board is really no longer an issue. Instead, invite only the best to be on your board and allow technology to facilitate your communication.

Sales Tip!

As you invite each member to participate, be very clear about your expectations for each person, the frequency with which you plan to consult and how, and your need for balanced, honest feedback. After each person agrees, discuss how each member would like to be compensated for their time and expertise. In most cases, a trade or barter is performed for goods or services, and, sometimes (depending on the unique relationship), a small gift or favor is enough. If necessary, offer to pay a small fee, as the value of the board's feedback will be returned many, many times over.

Techniques for Jumpstarting Your New Approach

Seek and exchange ideas. Routinely seek information on different topics— in journals, magazines, the Internet, and through associations. Share those ideas with your colleagues and customers to build confidence and credibility.

Share success. Create opportunities to share news of your successes with others— not only large, noteworthy ones but also smaller ones whose value is greater than their total sum. Build a support network by reporting on that challenging cold call, the super game of catch that you just had with your child, or any other success that had a formative impact on you.

Use relaxation/meditation. Sit comfortably, eyes closed (if you prefer). Breathe slowly and deeply. Visualize a pleasing, restful place. As thoughts enter your mind, let them come and go and anchor yourself with calming phrases. Practice for several minutes (5-10) as often as possible.

Smile (and laugh, if possible) at least 25 times per day. Count each time until smiling becomes a habit . . . . even and especially during difficulty times. Watch, and soon you'll be at 25 before 10 a.m.!

Quick Techniques for Reigniting a Plateaued Sales Career

You don't have to wait for your new habits to take effect to begin seeing results. Try some of the following strategies:

1.　　Try role-playing over the phone.

2.   Read a minimum of one sales book, journal, or newsletter each month.

3.   Attend every seminar your organization offers.

4.   Join local professional or trade organizations.

5.   Set higher goals for yourself with realistic time frames.

6.   Participate vigorously in every sales contest your company hosts.

7.   Ask to participate in ad hoc problem-solving sessions regarding major concerns.

8.   Ask for new assignments or trainings and challenge yourself with novel products or services.

9.   Assign yourself to special task forces or focus groups to become a company expert on a niche trade or industry.

10.   Volunteer to help train new sales representatives.

11.   Ask to be sent on a college recruitment visit.

12.   Work with a professional career counselor.

Chapter 12 Summary

Careers don't burn out, but even the best professionals can. If you find yourself feeling unmotivated or depressed because of a stalled sales career, then consider that the source could actually stem from within. Learn and apply strategies for getting back on track and to fulfill your true potential in the field:

1. Take a pledge to change yourself. No one can change you, and you can't change anyone else.

2. Create your own board of directors. Think of this personal board as your 'inner circle,' or, quite possibly, those confidants who harbor the most important information about your personal and professional life and, therefore, best understand you and your goals.

www.ingramcontent.com/pod-product-compliance
Lightning Source LLC
Chambersburg PA
CBHW060617210326
41520CB00010B/1376